WHEREVER
YOU ARE

COME OUT, WHEREVER YOU ARE

THE GREAT ESCAPE IN WALES

Herbert Williams

gomer

First Impression – 2004
Second Impression – 2004

ISBN 1 84323 199 9

© Herbert Williams

Herbert Williams has asserted his right under the
Copyright, Designs and Patents Act, 1988,
to be identified as Author of this Work.

First published by Quartet Books Ltd 1976

Printed in Wales at
Gomer Press, Llandysul, Ceredigion SA44 4JL

To my late parents –

Richard David Williams
and
Minnie Esther Williams

PREFACE

This is the story of the biggest escape of German prisoners of war from any camp in Britain in World War Two. It is a remarkable tale which, like all Great Escapes, has captured the public imagination. Even so, when this book was first published by Quartet in 1976, I little thought that interest in it would continue into a new century. Although it has been out of print for many years, scarcely a month passes without my getting a few letters or emails from people searching for copies. I have had to reply that, regrettably, I haven't a clue where they might find them. There have even been times when I have been without a copy myself, because to lend a book to someone is often to say goodbye to it for ever. In my darker moments I have imagined myself one day standing in the shoes of that pathetic old author in the TV ad, going through Yellow Pages and ringing up bookshops who may possibly have a copy of his immortal book on angling. Well, I have been spared that by Gomer's decision to bring out this new edition. Blessings on them.

I have resisted the temptation to tinker with the text, because the facts remain the same. This means the occasional anachronism, such as the reference to police patrol cars as 'pandas' in the first chapter. When this book first came out, the sight of cops chasing around everywhere in their little panda cars was still a novelty. I hope such things will only add to the interest of this reprint instead of taking away from it.

I wrote the book as a spin-off from the TV documentary *Come Out, Come Out Wherever You Are*, in which I was involved as researcher. This was a joint venture between BBC Wales and NDR, a company in what was then West Germany. I must again acknowledge my indebtedness to those without whom my book could not have been written – not least the late Superintendent William C. May of the Glamorgan Constabulary, a policeman of the old school whose courage and efficiency were matched only by his courtesy. Sadly, my co-researcher Brenda Thomas of BBC Wales is no longer with us, either, and neither is Jack Wiggins, former editor of the *South Wales Echo*, for whom I wrote a series of articles on the escape and its aftermath. Others who gave me invaluable support and assistance include Gareth Price, former Controller, BBC Wales and now Director of the Thomson Foundation; Piers Jessop, who directed *Come Out, Come Out Wherever You Are*; Geoffrey Rich, editor of the *South Wales Echo* at the time my book was first published; Herbert Phillips and Christian Herrendoerfer of NDR; and six of the ex-prisoners who escaped from Island Farm – Hans Harzheim, Werner Zielasko, Helmhart Perl, Hermann Schallenberg, Karl Ludwig and Carl-Heinz Brockmeyer.

To these must be added the names of those who have assisted me in bringing out this new edition: Neil Sumner, of the Environmental and Planning Services Directorate, Bridgend CBC, and his colleague Rob Jones; Menna Richards, Controller, BBC Wales; Liz

Veasey, Research and Archive Sales Co-ordinator, BBC Wales; Tony Woolway, Chief Librarian of the Western Mail and Echo Ltd, and his assistant Edwina Turner; my brother Richard Williams, for research at the Newspaper Library in Colindale, London; Bryn Jones, Local Studies Librarian, Cardiff CBC; the staff of Bridgend Library and Information Service; photographer David Williams; Frank and Joan Knights; Byron Rogers, for permission to quote extracts from his article *'The Great Escape … in Wales',* in the August 2001 number of Saga magazine; and Ceri Wyn Jones, English-language Editor, and Mairwen Prys Jones, Publishing Director, of Gomer Press.

Above all, my thanks are due to the scores of people who shared their memories of the escape with me, and to my wife Dorothy and my family for their unfailing encouragement and support.

Come out, come out, wherever you are.
I know, I know you're not very far . . .

1940s song

ONE

Garfield Davies had an unexpected audience when ploughing one of his fields on a fine spring day in 1945. Groups of German prisoners of war gazed intently at his efforts through the barbed wire that encircled Island Farm camp just outside Bridgend, a small town in a rural part of Glamorgan. He thought they were admiring the straightness of his furrows and, with a mixture of individual pride and patriotic zeal, he handled his tractor with particular care to show them that a Welsh farmer had as much skill as anyone the Third Reich could produce.

A few days later, however, he realized that for all they cared he could have been doing a figure eight on the tractor. Their only concern had been that he should not be clumsy enough to dislodge a large stone he had noticed propped up against a grass bank just outside the wire.

That stone had concealed the exit from a sixty-foot tunnel which had been dug under the wire. And it was through this tunnel that sixty-seven prisoners crawled to freedom on the night of 10-11 March.

This was the biggest escape of Germans from any POW camp in Britain during the Second World War, and it resulted in a massive manhunt involving spotter planes hedge-hopping over the placid acres of the Vale of Glamorgan and civilians enthusiastically joining in the game of hunt-the-Jerry. There were some extraordinary moments, such as when two respectable schoolteachers talking to each other in Welsh in a Cardiff hotel were mistaken for Germans on the run! Farmer Dilwyn Martin took the precaution of carrying a twelve-bore shotgun on his tractor for a couple of days, and two sisters living on a lonely farm on Margam Mountain put out food at night for the prisoners they knew were hiding in the bracken to dissuade them from breaking into their farmhouse.

The events of the seven days that elapsed between the time the first prisoners escaped and the last were back behind the wire throw an interesting light on wartime attitudes. Although, with hindsight, we can see that the war in Europe had only eight weeks to run, at the time people had a different perspective. The Allies had advanced to the Rhine in the west and the Oder in the east, but had still to launch the spring offensive that finally crushed Hitler. In the Far East, the Japanese counter-attack in Burma was causing heavy British casualties, the vital capture of Okinawa – which war historians have colourfully described as the 'inner gateway' to Japan – had still to be effected, and the suicidal exploits of the Kamikaze pilots provided depressing evidence that the warriors of Emperor Hirohito were ready to resist to their last drop of blood. Moreover the Germans in Camp 198 – the official designation of Island Farm – were, in a sense, insulated by their captivity. They had been there since the previous November, when they had defiantly sung their old fighting songs as they were formed up outside Bridgend railway station and marched to the camp just over a mile away. Shut away from the world in that compound, many of them still clung defiantly to the hope of ultimate victory for the Führer. For some, however, this mass escape was simply a sporting adventure, a relief from the crushing boredom of captivity.

Whatever the motives of the men who risked death by crawling under the wire (for the guards had orders to shoot once their warning cry was ignored), there is no doubt that their tunnel was a masterpiece of its kind. It was shored in approved mining fashion with uprights and cross-sections of timber, and had an air-line ingeniously constructed out of scores of condensed-milk tins strung end to end after their tops and bottoms had been removed. This was wedged into a bucket and air was forced through by means of a four-blade fan made out of tin and operated by hand. The escapers took with them iron rations, including corned beef and biscuits, and a plentiful supply of cigarettes. They also carried makeshift compasses with magnetized razor-blades serving as arrows and, in some cases, the base of the compass was obtained by stuffing an empty Vaseline tin with chewed-up bread which dried hard as stone. Maps showing railway lines and ports were drawn on handkerchiefs and scarves, and one enterprising officer even used the tail of his shirt for this purpose!

The escape was planned down to the last detail, but it did not take the authorities wholly by surprise. Only a month earlier another tunnel had been discovered in the course of construction, and the camp staff had been expecting trouble ever since this batch of prisoners had arrived in the murk of a late November evening. They were nearly all officers, and far more belligerent than the other ranks who had been there previously. Island Farm was not the best place for them, because it was not a purpose-built camp but a hastily modified barracks originally intended to house the workers at a munitions factory only a mile away. The official thinking had been that the women, many of whom lived twenty or thirty miles away, would not wish to travel long distances through the blackout day after day, but like so much official thinking it took no account of human psychology. There were housewives with homes to run as best they could while their men were at war, and even the unmarried girls preferred to go home at the end of their shift rather than endure the misery of life in a barracks. So the concrete huts remained forlorn and deserted until the authorities at last found some use for them by billeting American soldiers there just before D-Day. Nothing like the Yanks had ever hit Bridgend before, and the town was agog when the news got around that General Eisenhower had visited the camp in person to give a pep talk to the troops. It was delivered, typically, from the back of a truck in the parade ground, and when he gestured to the lined-up troops to gather round they broke ranks and cheered him wildly, waving their caps in the air at his final assertion that they were 'gonna hit the hell out of the Jerries!' With morale so high, Dwight must have thought the battle half-won already. Soon afterwards the Americans left for their secret destinations along the south coast of England, and as they joined the assault on Hitler's Continental defences in the summer of 1944 the huts where they had plastered their pin-ups of Dorothy Lamour and Betty Grable were taken over by medically downgraded British troops whose role in the war was less dramatic. They had the task of converting Island Farm into a prisoner-of-war camp in readiness for the huge influx of Germans into the country, which the War Cabinet confidently expected to result from the Allied invasion. Some of the huts were ear-marked for prisoners, others for guards, and the soldiers, fed up and far from home, set about the boring task of unwinding roll after roll of barbed wire and erecting acetylene flares at various points along the perimeter. Camp 198 was still so insecure when the first bedraggled prisoners of war arrived, however, that the captives themselves were compelled to put up the perimeter wire and ground towers under the direction of the guards, who were armed with rifles and bayonets. They were a mixed bag of Italian and German soldiers, plus a few German railway officials who had been picked up in France by American troops and sent to Britain as POWs. When the camp was reasonably secure the guards played cards, smoked their Woodbines and wondered when the hell the war was going to end so that they could all pack up and go home.

Their troubles, however, were just beginning. They

had still to endure the young German officers who, from the start, set out to taunt and annoy their British captors.

Their arrival was supposed to be a well-kept secret, but in a small town like Bridgend nothing stays secret for long. As the word got around that hordes of grey-uniformed Nazis were pouring on to the platform, crowds hurried to the station to share in the excitement. The noise was itself enough to rouse the whole town, for the Germans had the audacity to sing their national anthem 'Deutschland Uber Alles' as they were formed up by the harrassed and heavily outnumbered military and police. The tightness of the security at the station came as a surprise to many of the Island Farm guards because they had not been warned that these prisoners were of a very different calibre from those who had pre-ceded them. 'No civilian was allowed anywhere near them, and when I saw the prisoners I knew why,' said former guard Fred Allsop. 'They were nearly all officers, and all the way to the camp they sang "Marching to England" and "We Will Fight and Die for the Führer".'

They came, in fact, not like defeated men but like conquerors. They swaggered about the platform, staring insolently at their captors, and in bearing and appearance they were, considering their status, almost indecently smart. 'The prisoners were well clad for the cold of that winter, and had obviously dressed in their best uniforms and packed their suitcases and kitbags before surrendering or being captured', recalled the late

James Fitzpatrick, who was a police inspector at Bridgend at the time. 'Their bearing and swagger was far removed from the popular conception of the cowed and captured prisoner.' Another senior police officer reflected: 'I remember thinking to myself – if this were an invading force, they'd set about us all right!'

In spite of the tight cordon outside the station, one woman broke through to show her hatred of the enemy in the most positive way open to her. She spat in the face of a German officer, and then disappeared into the crowd. This was exactly the kind of incident the police wished to avoid, and they were relieved when it provoked nothing more than a contemptuous grin on the face of the officer. Although outwardly the police displayed the calm and resolution expected of them, privately they had grave doubts about what might happen on the mile-long march between the station and the camp. The streets, normally deserted at night, were now filling up with townspeople eager to taste the excitement of such a radical break in wartime routine, and they were grimly aware that some of the onlookers would have lost relatives in the war. They feared that open hostility might inflame the Germans into retaliation; they also feared that some of the captives, seeing that the size of their escort was barely the minimum required, might break and run for it.

In the event, there was no trouble. The Germans marched proudly through the streets, keeping step and singing martial songs, and the people on the pavements watched them in silence and kept their thoughts to themselves. As the last of the long grey column of men passed under the flares into Camp 198, James Fitzpatrick and his colleagues breathed sighs of relief. The first ordeal was over. But the real test was still to come.

By a strange chance, the route from the station to the camp took the Germans past the home of the man who, more than anyone else, had applied himself to the task of deciding what should be done if they ever managed to escape. He was Superintendent William May, a thoughtful and philosophical police officer proud of the traditions of the Glamorgan Constabulary and determined to uphold them whatever the challenge. The presence of 1,600 prisoners of war on his doorstep posed new and special problems of law and order, and he would need all his knowledge of men and their motives as well as his flair for organization to cope with them.

Bill May's closest associates outside the police force in devising such a scheme were the camp commandant, Lieutenant-Colonel Edwin Darling, M.C., and Brigadier Birch, commander of the South Wales Light Infantry Brigade. Darling, who was fifty-one, was reaching the end of his army career. He had served out east and with his courteous manners and insistence that officers were also gentlemen could fairly be described as one of the old brigade. Since he had escaped back to Britain from a POW camp in Germany in the First World War, he was well versed in the tricks of would-be escapers.

When the crunch came, however, he did not at once grasp the scale of the escape and a senior German officer thought him ingenuous.

The South Wales Light Infantry Brigade had its headquarters in Abergavenny, a market town forty miles north-east of Bridgend in a serene stretch of countryside where, to the north, the green folds of the Black Mountains enclosed such pearls as the ruins of Llanthony Abbey, and the industrial valleys of Monmouthshire furrowed south to the sea with their legacy of bitter class conflict. When the war began the HQ had been at Porthcawl, a seaside resort on the shores of the Bristol Channel, but with the threat of invasion it had been thought impolitic to have the strategic nerve-centre so near the coast, and the Home Guard had been entrusted with the immediate defence of the beaches. By this stage of the war, with the Allies poised for the final knock-out, the tank traps and observation posts along the coast looked as redundant as the Martello towers of the Napoleonic wars, so the only security problem that troubled Brigadier Birch was that of the POW camps. Island Farm was the largest in his area, and the truculence of many of its inmates suggested that it might not be long before the paper plan he had helped to work out would be forced to prove itself in a real-life situation.

An event in Germany the year before strongly influenced the thinking of Birch, Darling and May. In March 1944 forty-seven Allied officers had been shot after taking part in a mass-escape from Stalag Luft III, a deed condemned by a German general after the war as 'sheer murder'. They were determined that there should be no wholesale shooting in Wales, either by accident or design. Birch thus emphasized the importance of the civil police in any search for escaped prisoners. Indeed, he ruled that if it appeared likely that no prisoner was more than three miles from the camp the operation was to be left entirely to the police, unless a serious collapse of law and order made the intervention of the military absolutely essential. If an escape involved a search within a five-mile radius the police would be reinforced by Home Guard operating as special constables and, like the police, bearing firearms only in special circumstances. 'Beyond this', in the words of Superintendent May, 'the sky was the limit, with Brigadier Birch in full command.'

In calculating which plan should be put into operation, the vital consideration was the time that had elapsed between the breakout and its discovery. Naturally, the longer the lapse of time, the greater the number of prisoners likely to be involved and the further they would have travelled. There were fears that the men on the run might contact enemy agents in the form of local quislings, and the authorities were keenly aware that in the vicinity of Bridgend there were ample opportunities for sabotage. Within a mile of the camp was that munitions factory at Waterton, where 39,000 people worked round the clock providing the firepower for the assault on Hitler's heartland. There were airfields at St Athan, Llandow and Stormy Down, all within ten miles of Island Farm, and several collieries just to the north, where the dark fingers of the South Wales coalfield touched the fringe of the agricultural Vale of Glamorgan. The legendary Rhondda, one of the greatest coal-producing areas in the world, was only a dozen miles away. No wonder that behind their outward show of cool self-confidence the army brass hats and senior police officers were profoundly uneasy.

A large map in code was prepared, setting out the points of strategic importance so that in the event of an escape a rough pattern might be identified which could lead to a widespread plan of disruption and destruction being nipped in the bud. The humble village bobby had a vital role to play, and so did the ordinary civilian. As soon as the Germans arrived at Island Farm, the village constables toured the local farms on their bicycles warning farmers to be on the look-out for anything unusual, such as strangers on their land or discarded belongings. Even the theft of farm implements, or a sign that hay-lofts had been slept in overnight, could provide vital clues. 'The essence of the scheme was that if anything happened, everybody was to know about it,' said Bill May. 'The co-operation of the public was absolutely vital.'

Consultation of this kind was nothing new in itself, for in those days, when the word panda signified only a strange animal in the zoo, the police placed great reliance on personal contact with the public. In country areas particularly, reliable citizens would act as unofficial detectives, passing on tip-offs to the village

21

policeman, who was himself an integral part of the community. The constable would cover his beat by bicycle, meeting up with his colleagues from neighbouring areas at set points to find out if all was well and to pass on information as required. With the arrival of the POWs at Island Farm, the system was refined so that in every village and hamlet there were human 'observation posts' trained to keep their eyes skinned for anything that could spell trouble.

A divisional circular signed by Superintendent May emphasized that the scheme would be worthless without the individual alertness of the man on the beat. 'He should be a complete organization unto himself within the larger plan, forming one of the integral parts of it; manifesting initiative and the readiness to accept responsibility,' runs the circular. It goes on:

> The prisoners are highly trained military personnel and would practise military field technique to its fullest extent, and it is to meet and defeat this that the policeman should set himself. This, of course, is something different from the usual police routine but in the efficient policeman the alert mind is always receptive to new ideas. If its alertness is tuned up to the right pitch it will be able to grasp new situations quickly and carefully work out and apply what is to the best advantage in all emergencies.
>
> First of all, it should be recognized that the escaping prisoner has opportunities for sabotage in abundance in this division. Therefore the method of dealing with the hunt and capture of escapees will

necessarily have to be considered on its merits in the light of the circumstances as they are likely to arise in each case. The informants constituting information points on the respective beats should be encouraged to repeatedly search and examine their premises and to keep an active observation on all points. When reporting any information every detail should be included; particularly the location of suspects; approximate number; whether the prisoners are on the move or static and whether their attitude as far as it can be observed is merely one of avoiding capture or of violently resisting recapture.

A constant search patrol should be maintained, linking up with the various military points, furnishing the military personnel with all possible information collected in the course of the patrol and from the information points . . .

Immediately following a report of an escape, all pedestrians and motorists not known to the police should be called upon to produce their identity cards and upon being proved correct they should be warned of the escape and their co-operation sought by reporting the movements of any suspicious persons or incident on their journeys to the police.

Whilst there is now no legal obligation there is still a moral obligation on the part of the public, particularly on the occasion of a mass escape of prisoners of war, to immobilize cars, cycles, lorries and any other vehicle. Failure to act promptly in this respect will give the escaped prisoners the chance to provide themselves with transport from unattended vehicles or vehicles in insecure garages. It would be all to the good if the readily removable parts could be taken away from the vehicle for the time being.

The prisoner's greatest advantage against his pursuers will be his highly developed military instinct to adopt all forms of subterfuge. To beat him, one must have a perfect knowledge of the countryside and be able to find one's way about just as well by night and in fog as in broad daylight. To attain this the pursuers should have the qualities of:

(a) a good hunter;
(b) be able to improvise and make quick decisions;
(c) never to tire when following up information received;
(d) suspect everything;
(e) always be on the alert;
(f) once the alarm of an escape is given, to reconnoitre unceasingly.

This expressive circular, which stylistically typified Bill May's enthusiasm for something more literary than mere officialese, was sent to all police stations in C division. It was dated 26 December 1944.

TWO

There were no more quiet nights for anyone within earshot of Island Farm now. The Nazis' lusty rendering of the 'Horst Wessel' and other rousing choruses could be heard not only in the heart of Bridgend but in the tiny, picture-postcard village of Merthyr Mawr, which with its thatched cottages and air of timeless repose stood between the prison camp and the nearby sand-dunes. But it wasn't just the singing that woke the babies and frightened the nervous. Sometimes the prisoners would howl and shriek like men in the grip of an ungovernable terror, and when the mood took them they would bang their cutlery on the tables for minutes on end in an unholy percussion. The patience of the guards was sorely tested, and so was that of the local people, who consoled themselves with the thought that it was only the resounding successes of the Allies that had brought such unwelcome strangers into their midst. All the same, the sight of these young warriors being marched along the open roads on their daily exercises, albeit under the watchful eyes of their guards, was a thoroughly unpleasant one for many of the people who had to suffer it. 'They'd look at you as if you were dirt', one housewife recalled. And Ted Spencer, who used to be the village policeman in Laleston, remembers them staring up at the sign 'County Police' outside the station and muttering among themselves. 'A lot of people resented them coming round here exercising because they didn't like the look of them', he said. 'They wondered what would happen if they ran wild.'

Even hardened soldiers could be overwhelmed by the sight of so many of the enemy milling around. A wartime commando who had faced German fire without flinching at Dieppe and Narvik still looks puzzled and disconcerted as he tries to explain his behaviour when he came home on leave one night. 'I had to walk past the camp on my way home from the station,' he said, 'but when I got there I couldn't move. I just stood on the other side of the road, petrified. It was the thought of so many of them crowded in there, I suppose. It was different from fighting them out in the open . . . I felt somehow they could get through that wire easily. One of the guards saw me standing there and got a bit suspicious. He wondered what I was up to. In fact he came across and asked me for identification. I told him what was wrong and in the end he walked past the camp with me.' More than thirty years on, the memory still troubled him. 'I can't explain it. I don't suppose I ever will.'

Inside the camp there were the inevitable divisions and tensions. There was the basic difference in outlook between the older officers who were all for a quiet life, and the bellicose young Nazis who were out to cause as much trouble as possible. For them, it was a matter of pride. They felt their honour besmirched by being taken prisoner, and to submit meekly to captivity was a humiliation they could not endure. They found it hard to admit even to themselves that Germany was on the brink of defeat, and it was certainly impossible to admit it to others. Those who publicly voiced any doubts in the Führer did so at their peril, as a middle-aged prisoner called Otto Iskat discovered to his cost late in January. He made some casual remarks about the futility of war, and was found the next morning lying exhausted on his bed in a state of shock. What exactly happened will never be known, but the manhandling he received at the hands of his 'comrades' sent him to his grave within days.

In their own words, this was a camp of 'one-hundred-and-fifty-percenters'. Most of these young officers were Nazi to the core, and they took a delight in reaching through their prison bars to twist the tail of the British lion. They shamelessly duped the commandant, persuading him that since he was short of personnel they genuinely wished to play their part in the smooth running of the camp. They offered to take over the administration of the account cards, the system by which prisoners obtained their quota of cigarettes, toothpaste, razor-blades and so on from the canteen. Lieutenant Colonel Darling agreed at once, not realizing that this was simply a device enabling the more ardent Nazis to victimize and intimidate men they considered politically unreliable. Instead of giving them the goods, they kept them for themselves. They also persuaded Darling that they needed more exercise, and put forward a plan for a sports arena complete with pit for practising the long jump and high jump. Impressed with their initiative, and keen to see them occupying themselves harmlessly, he gave his approval, not suspecting that their real intention in digging the pit was to conceal the soil from their tunnelling operations.

There were, however, two tunnels at Island Farm. One of them was discovered fortuitously in January by two officers who had been attached to the camp for a few days before moving on elsewhere. They were told to 'look around the huts' because nobody quite knew what to do with them, but being eager young types they took the assignment seriously and gave the startled prisoners – who were not used to seeing their custodians inside the compound on a Saturday after-noon – some hard looks. They inspected the huts pretty thoroughly too, and much to their surprise found a tell-tale ring of dust around the concrete hearth-stone in front of a stove. Brushing it aside, they discovered with mounting excitement that the stone had been cut away, and when they raised it the shaft of a tunnel was revealed. As they waited triumphantly for the commandant and adjutant to arrive they noticed that the prisoner they had turfed out of his bunk in order to search the hut was lingering in the doorway looking worried but they did not attach much significance to this. It soon became clear, however, that he had good cause for alarm because one of his comrades was still in the tunnel. It was Darling who spotted a movement in the darkness as he squatted on his haunches staring into the shaft. 'There's somebody down there!' he exclaimed, and at that the prisoner in the doorway rushed forward jabbering excitedly and waving his arms. The man underground, who had been working naked on the tunnel face, was hauled up just in time, for he was black in the face with grime and near suffocation. It turned out that his friend on the bunk had been supplying him with air by means of a primitive fan.

According to Inspector Fitzpatrick, who years later recalled a conversation with Darling, the commandant was wise enough in the ways of POWs to know that his troubles were only just beginning. 'We must now be more alert than ever,' he quoted Darling as saying. 'Tunnels are never dug singly. There are always two going on at the same time, so that if one is found its discovery may lull the camp staff into a feeling of complacency.'

This sense of urgency, however, was not adequately conveyed to the guards. 'Having discovered, as we had planned, the diversionary tunnel,' said one of the German officers in the hut where the successful escape began, 'the Tommies thought they had foiled the planned operation.'

To be fair to the despised Tommies though, they did not have the easiest of tasks. It was a thankless job patrolling the wire at Island Farm at the best of times. There were no raised cat-walks to make life easier for the guards, nor were there any searchlights to fix any would-be escaper in their accusing and irresistible glare.

At first the guards had trudged unhappily through the mud beyond the outer ring of barbed wire, but later they had been provided with a clinker path and finally, almost luxuriously, with duckboards. But the lighting was still primitive at the time of the escape, consisting of acetylene flares about five feet off the ground. They were arranged in pairs around the camp perimeter and arguably gave more help to the prisoners than they did to the guards, for while they enabled the prisoners to see exactly where the guard was, the men patrolling the wire complained that they distorted their vision. They were, in the words of former guard Ronald Whalley, 'a disgrace'. Another, more unexpected, difficulty was posed by the presence of so many sheep in the fields around the camp. 'They coughed just like a man,' he said. 'It could be very deceptive.'

Apart from the possibility of shooting a sheep in the mistaken idea that it was an escaping German, there was the psychological problem posed by the knowledge that there were so many eyes on you as you went about your repetitious and wearisome task. At best those eyes were indifferent; at worst they were hostile and contemptuous. Moreover, the prisoners knew that they were more than a match for their guards, and the guards were aware of this. The young officers inside the compound prided themselves on being the cream of the German army, whereas the men outside were medically downgraded by reason of illness or injury and best described, in the words of a senior police officer searching for a charitable description, as 'first-class

Dad's Army'. Their duties, however, would have demoralized much better men. 'You was either on guard or you was on fire duty or you was on fatigues or you was on jankers,' recalled one of them wearily, the disenchantment still obvious despite the passage of three decades. Indeed, they had their own escape hole in a hedge through which they fled via their billet windows while on jankers 'for a couple of pints in Bridgend and back again'. When the men were in drink there were often fights, and the fact that they were thrown together from so many different regiments did not help. But in March 1945 the military could not afford to be choosy. With every fit man fighting in the various theatres of war, they were hard pressed to find the soldiers to guard the thousands of prisoners who were being rounded up as the Allies advanced triumphantly through Europe. 'We were handicapped by the fact that our soldiers were all the dregs from the depots,' said a retired major, whose frankness of speech can be attributed to a certain bluff honesty rather than to vindictiveness. 'They had to search the depots to find 200 or 300 chaps to come down. There was no question of the *esprit de corps* of a regiment. They were chaps who were sick or wounded – we had to take anyone. And they had a most wretched job. You had to do what you could to boost morale up.'

The prisoners and the guards inhabited two separate worlds, in more senses than one. Contact was minimal. The prisoners had their own cooks to prepare their food, and their own camp leader to maintain liaison between

31

themselves and the British authorities. Security demanded a daily counting of heads and random searches of huts, but for the most part the British stayed outside the compound and the prisoners were, within the limits of their captivity, a self-governing community. They also impressed their captors by the way they maintained the military virtue of good cheer in the face of adversity. 'They were very good singers,' recalled the ex-major. 'They used to form up for meals and march to the dining-room, singing as they went. Remarkable singing. They were German national songs, I suppose. There was no question of them being depressed. On their way to meals they were in a proper column. Very smart lot of chaps.

'The routine of the camp was that after breakfast they had to parade in hut formations at nine o'clock, for the morning count. We knew how many people should be in each hut. The orderly officer would go into the compound with the sergeant-major and NCOs and various men, and they'd count the prisoners. But they had to be careful that none of the men dodged from one hut to another. They spoofed us once or twice when one or two chaps got out. Some went from one group to another to disguise the fact that someone was missing. When all the hut counts were brought to the chief officer they were added up and if we didn't get the right number we kept them on parade until the odd chap was found around the camp.

'The interesting thing about it is that we felt at one time they knew which hut was going to be specially searched. How it was known we don't know – whether it came from one of our chaps or not . . . We searched one hut every morning. When it was selected the prisoners were marched off to the concert hall. They were stripped and searched there, while the officers and NCOs went through everything in the hut – clothes, beds, everything. And they tapped the concrete floor with iron bars. We looked especially for any kind of clothing which had earth or soil and only when the hut had been properly searched were the people allowed to come back in. In the light of subsequent events these Germans were too clever for us in many ways, because even when this tunnelling was going on we never found any suggestions of soiled clothing.'

He recalls that, from the very start, these officers insisted on their rights. 'They wanted better accommodation than the other ranks who had been there before them. They created a fuss because they had to sleep on straw palliasses for a little while. According to the Geneva Convention we had to produce sheets for the officers. The other ranks had been content with the straw. The officers were very cocky chaps, very arrogant. At least the younger ones were – the older ones were glad to be taken prisoner. But the younger ones were arrogant in every way. I believe their one desire was to prove their manhood by escaping, or trying to escape. But they had nothing to complain of in their conditions. I think they had better arrangements for food and accommodation than the chaps guarding them. We were not terribly comfortable as officers ourselves.

'I don't think we had any proof of any prisoners victimizing other prisoners. I believe once or twice in the night there were thuds and bangs in the huts but we never went into the compound at night if we could help it. We only went in when we had an idea that something was afoot. This irritated the prisoners a lot at two o'clock in the morning, I can tell you! It was a different count then from the daily one. They had to go through a narrow gate between two compounds, with two officers counting them as they went.'

There was a curious episode which reveals not only the negative attitude which the authorities adopted at this time towards the political arguments inside the compounds, but the degree of tolerance they showed their prisoners. With the approach of Hitler's birthday, the more zealous young Nazis decided to send him greetings. This quickly extended to a decision that *every* prisoner in the camp should send the Führer a birthday card. The older officers objected, but fell into line when taunted with being unpatriotic and sucking up to the British. Surprisingly, the camp staff allowed the cards to be posted to Germany. 'They either made them themselves,' said the second-in-command at Island Farm, 'or bought them through the camp purchasing officer.'

To the authorities, the prisoners were roughly divided into the young and not-so-young, but the Germans themselves naturally saw things in different terms. 'There were two main groups in my opinion,' said one of them, looking back thirty years. 'There was one group –

and you could find them among the younger ones as well as the older men – who went into a kind of phlegmatic state. You'd have men who just lay on their bunks the whole day, ostensibly in order to save calories. And you had another group which became active.'

The activities took various forms. There were those who turned to craftwork, making *objets d'art* out of empty tins, while others attended lectures which a former professor of law gave while sitting on his bunk with his 'students' gathered around. 'By God,' recalled one of them, 'we took everything in because one suddenly realized that in actual fact the grey cells were still there! And what struck me as phenomenal is that these university teachers could pass on their enormous knowledge simply from memory.'

There was a camp magician whose dry motto was 'often imitated, never equalled', and a Luftwaffe pilot who miraculously produced a gramophone with a single record – of Mozart's *Eine Kleine Nachtmusik*. 'In the evening,' said one of his grateful comrades, 'everybody lay in bed, listening to it. That was a unique experience for us.'

A camp theatre was started by Herbert Baumann, now a successful architect in Cologne, and the sportsmen caught the eye of the guards with their prowess at volleyball and soccer. But all these were mere palliatives, not cures for the sense of oppression with captivity that strengthened daily in the more active men. There was only one way to overcome that completely and that was to quit the camp altogether.

THREE

The construction of a sixty-foot tunnel entails a lot of hard, dangerous, disagreeable work. There is the tough physical graft, the feeling of claustrophobia, the fear of being buried alive. In spite of this, there was no shortage of volunteers when the word got around that the boys in Hut 9 were digging a tunnel. The difficulty was keeping some control of the numbers, for if a mass escape is to succeed it must be meticulously planned and involve only those men who can be relied on implicitly.

Most of the escapers were under thirty, but there were some men in their forties who eagerly joined the ranks with an enthusiasm that outmatched their discretion. When it came to acting the part of human moles, many of them were unfit for the task. This put greater pressure on their younger comrades, who shrugged their shoulders and assumed total responsibility for the tunnelling. They called themselves the worker bees, and prided themselves on the combination of brain and fist they brought to the job.

Very few, if any, had done this kind of work before, and their callowness showed in their assumption at first that because the heavy clay beneath the surface was so hard to excavate, the walls of the tunnel would hold up on their own. They were quickly disillusioned when lumps of clay and rocks tumbled on the backs of a digging party one day, an alarming experience which convinced them that they would have to adopt proper mining techniques. The word went around the camp, and several men came forward to provide the know-how – although to this day many of the escapers do not know who they were because they didn't bother to ask. 'We just did what we were told,' said Werner Zielasko, who is now a beer wholesaler.

One of the first essentials was to find timber, and there was plenty of it around. Benches were stolen from the canteen and sawn up to provide supports for the tunnel sides and roof, and since they were made of oak or beech they proved ideal for the purpose. Another essential was tools, and here again the Germans obtained without much difficulty an iron spike and a short-handled shovel. An improvised skid for hauling away the earth was constructed, with 'ropes' made out of electric-light wire and stirrup-pump tubing. Blankets and dungarees were draped over the tunnel sides to lessen the danger of carrying soil back to the hut, and most of the diggers made the risk minimal by working completely naked. Even so, there was a critical moment when a guard found a shirt covered with soil in one of the huts. The prisoners, cool and plausible, laughed it off as a relic of the escape attempt which had been nipped in the bud, and he was so thoroughly taken in that he failed to report it to his senior officers – including, of course, the major who remains convinced that 'no suggestion' of soiled clothing had been found at Island Farm.

The problem of soil disposal was even more acute now than before, because with the discovery of the first tunnel the Germans could no longer use the jumping pit. Some of it was taken outside the camp by prisoners who filled their pockets with earth and then surreptitiously scattered it while out walking under the supposedly watchful eyes of their guards, but clearly this was a method to be used only sparingly. The British camp staff were inclined to believe, after the event, that much of the soil went on the garden plots which some of the prisoners had in front of their huts, but while this was a convenient – and perhaps face-saving – explanation, it was nowhere near the truth of the matter. What really happened is that the Germans built a false wall under the very noses of the guards, and pushed the earth through to the other side. This wall covered what they termed a 'dead space' near the showers in the middle of the escape hut, a space designed perhaps for storage, but used for nothing in particular. The necessary bricks were not hard to come by, as there were plenty lying around the camp, and the wall was built one night while specially posted sentries kept watch. A brick was left loose so that it could be easily removed to enable the soil to be pushed through, and the audacious masons stepped back to survey their handiwork. It satisfied them, but would it fool the British? The answer came when the officers and NCOs next clumped through Hut 9 on a routine inspection. They hardly gave the wall a glance.

Jubilant with their success, the Germans pressed on with their tunnel with new zest. A sure sign of their progress was that now three men could work down there at a time. The man farthest in, hacking away at the face, piled the sledge with soil and shouted 'Pull!' when it was full, whereupon the second man allowed it to run through his legs to the third man in the roomy area directly below the shaft. Here the earth was put in kitbags and hauled to the surface, where it was kneaded into balls and dropped through the gap left by the loose brick into the space beyond.

The tunnel entrance was well disguised with the help of cement dust sprinkled around the edges of the removable stone, but there were inevitably some nasty moments. 'On one occasion the English camp commandant and the Intelligence officer were actually standing on the cover of the tunnel,' said Zielasko. 'The senior officer of the hut said his heart nearly stopped when he saw them!'

The diversion has a classic role in every POW escape, and Hut 9 had one in the form of glamorous women painted on the wall above the bunk where the tunnel began. They hoped the officers searching the hut would be more interested in admiring the artwork than thumping the concrete floor with their poles and iron bars, and so it proved. 'They were simply fascinated by these pretty ladies,' recalled one of the occupants of Hut 9 with a grin. 'They were less concerned about whether there might in actual fact be a hole in the floor.'

All this was good fun, but the tunnelling itself was

exhausting. 'When I joined in the work it was built half-way and by this time the air was very bad,' said Helmhart Perl, then a midshipman in the German Navy and now a lawyer in Dusseldorf. 'You could only work two or three minutes at a time.' It was at this stage that the air-line of condensed-milk tins was brought into use. It was wedged into a bucket, and the primitive four-blade fan was rotated with a handle to ventilate the tunnel. Apart from making the worker bees feel a good deal safer, this device increased their productivity dramatically. Instead of working only two minutes at a time, they could now go on for a quarter of an hour. Even so, the effort of will required to go into the tunnel was sometimes almost beyond their strength. 'It was always a real nightmare working in the tunnel,' confessed Perl. 'Up front at the face there was very little oxygen, despite the fact that we had a pipe, and after just a few minutes one's lungs were wheezing. Quite honestly I was frightened . . .' The tunnel was sprinkled with water so that the sledge would slide more easily along the ground, and the man at the face had an iron hook to gouge out the heavy clay, which was thickly embedded with stones. All the same it was back-breaking toil and it was only the constant cold showers they took that kept these amateur miners going.

They had the consolation, at least, of electric light to work by, for some old discarded cable was connected to the supply in the hut. One of the incidental problems concerned sleeping arrangements, for when a man from another hut was in a digging party he had to swap beds with a prisoner in Hut 9, as it was not safe to move about the camp at night: an illicit stroller might have given the whole game away.

The escapers were not all known to one another, but consisted essentially of individual groups of three, four or five people who came to hear that a tunnel was going ahead and asked if they could join in as well. 'We had considered how we should get out and then we learned that a tunnel was being built,' explained Perl. 'But today I couldn't even tell you who detailed me, who told me at any particular time that I had to work. I think the whole undertaking has to be seen from this standpoint. It was not really the concerted action of 100 or 200 people, but a large number of individual actions.' Nevertheless, those who had initiated the tunnel made sure they knew of the identity of each group, and they also worked out the order in which the groups should escape, depending on when they joined in the work. Thus Helmhart Perl, who was surprised to find that the tunnel was half-way to completion when he first went into it, was the sixty-fifth man to go through on the night of the escape. The very anonymity of the escapers was a protection against betrayal, for there was always the risk of someone tipping off the camp staff in order to pay off an old score – or simply to avoid the coals of fire which would surely be heaped on everyone else's head in the event of a mass escape. Thus each escape group knew for certain of the existence of only one or two other groups, and the obvious need for caution prevented anyone blabbing too loudly. The orders filtered down from above, and like good soldiers the men did not ask too many questions.

The tunnel took nearly three months to complete, and in its final stages the supply of timber ran dangerously low. It was then that someone had the brilliant idea of sawing through the legs of the bunk beds, and to make sure they were not of different heights all the beds in selected huts were shortened by exactly the same amount. This provided all the wood needed to complete the shoring of the tunnel, and with that crisis over the final arrangements went ahead. While each group had its own plan they shared a common pool of ideas. One of these was to toast white bread on the stoves in their huts until it was hard, and then to spice it, thus making it edible for several days. Some made weird and wonderful concoctions which would have given Mrs Beeton a brain storm, but in spite of all this scrimping and saving in order to build up a food store for the escape, they were increasingly worried that their rations might be inadequate. Apart from having enough to eat, however, they had to know where they were going. All the signposts had been removed from wartime Britain in case of invasion, so maps and compasses were an obvious necessity. The official mind, however, has its limitations, and the maps showing major railway lines and ports which used to adorn railway carriages had been left untouched. On their way to Bridgend the Germans had gleefully removed them with a future escape in mind, and now they set about copying them carefully. Paper was short, so some were drawn on toilet rolls, but other groups had more original ideas. There were maps beautifully sketched on white handkerchiefs, with the scale meticulously marked in the corner, while SS officer Karl Ludwig had a map, measuring nineteen inches by fifteen inches, drawn in ink on a shirt-tail. The spelling of the Welsh place names was erratic – 'Breckhock' for Brecknock and 'Harley' for Harlech – but no worse, perhaps, than the attempts of many Englishmen.

This disposed of the problem of maps, but what about compasses? The answer literally stared them in the face when they looked in their shaving mirrors – razor-blades which, when magnetized, served as directional arrows. They were stuck on the point of a pin, and obligingly pointed to magnetic north. The pin was embedded in a base which could be either a block of wood with a scooped-out centre or something more original, such as the bone-dry bread in a Vaseline tin.

So the big day drew closer, and the escapers thought of little else. Some were having second thoughts now, but it was too late to draw back. Fears which, until now, they had managed to suppress troubled their imaginations. Would they be shot while escaping? What would happen to them if they were caught? And the roof of their tunnel – their precious tunnel – might it finally collapse on them as they were crawling to freedom?

All this they kept to themselves. Outwardly they were calm, resourceful, sustained by their pride in themselves and their contempt for the guards they had duped all the way along the line. Their motives for escaping were mixed. Some, like Lieutenant Karl Ludwig, who had joined the military arm of the SS in 1936 at the age of eighteen and whose faith in Hitler was still strong, looked forward to fighting again in the victorious German Army. Others, aware that German cities lay in ruins after the heavy Allied bombing, were worried about the fate of their families and simply wished to get home. Many hoped to reach the republic of Ireland, which was neutral, so that they could return to Germany as soon as the war ended instead of waiting months or possibly years to be repatriated. And for some, the escape was simply an exhilarating adventure. 'There were no books in the camp at this time,' said Perl, who had been captured at Le Havre. 'Unless I have some activity it bothers me. I'd been a prisoner of war for six months and I was bored with the company of men all the time, seeing the same faces and hearing the same stories. That was reason enough to escape.' He resents the fact that when he was discharged his POW card bore the words 'Political escape' in bold red letters. 'I had no political motive,' he insists. 'It was just an adventure.'

Others were inspired chiefly by a sense of duty to their families. 'We thought they were expecting something of us,' said Werner Zielasko, with an honest effort to put himself back in the boots of the young man he had been thirty years ago. 'We had left our homes and our families with high hopes so we felt we had a duty to fulfil. Our pride had been hurt. We were angry

44

at being captured, angry at the bombing of our towns and cities. We felt we had to put up a fight, to show we wouldn't surrender. You must remember we were all products of an epoch. When Hitler came to power in 1933 we were boys of thirteen, fourteen and fifteen. We were tough guys, and we were proud of being tough. Our faith in Hitler had been shaken, especially after conversations with our older comrades, but you know – in a small corner of our hearts we still hoped Germany could win the war.'

FOUR

In the best tradition of POW escapes, the prisoners planned a diversion before the event and another on the night itself. On 7 March, two officers tried to cut their way through the wire and were caught in the act, according to plan. They used scissors cunningly made from an iron bedstead by the skilled smith who had earlier cut out the slab of concrete over the tunnel entrance with the aid of a red-hot chisel. Island Farm, like most POW camps, was rich in inventiveness.

This was the latest in a series of attempted escapes through the wire in February and early March. The idea was to put the camp staff off the scent of a tunnel, but they were never really anywhere near it. The prisoners, however, were leaving nothing to chance. One of their big worries was the presence of guard dogs between the inner and outer rings of barbed wire – mainly alsatians, but with a labrador thrown in for good measure. The zealousness of these hounds was such that the second-in-command at the camp, who regularly went the rounds of the wire at 11pm and 3am, feared they might take a chunk out of him before they put paid to any German. 'Hold the bloody dog still!' he used to shout to the handler when still some distance away.

Obviously something had to be done about those

dogs, and the answer came from the sergeant who was the leader of the German other ranks at Island Farm – who, in deference to the sense of military propriety which existed as strongly in captivity as on the battlefield, were kept separate from the officers. He suggested putting curry powder on the ground to deaden the dogs' sense of smell, an idea received at first with some scepticism by the escapers. Since they had nothing to lose, however, they decided to experiment, so on the morning of 10 March – D-Day for the Bridgend Germans – they scrounged some curry from their cooks and sprinkled it generously by the wire. The test would come when the alsatian passed by with its handler, going the rounds of the perimeter, for they meant to creep up on it to see if it still caught the scent in spite of the curry. They waited impatiently, then hid away at the dog's approach. As soon as it had gone by, they crept quietly up to the wire until they were within twenty-five yards of the animal, which continued on its way without turning a hair. They knew then that the experiment had succeeded, for normally the alsatian would catch the scent of a man at thirty-five yards.

The second diversion was the performance of a play in the camp theatre where the prisoners put on their own entertainments. As it turned out, this diversion was doubly necessary because on the eve of the escape the prisoners realized to their dismay that their doubts about the quantity of their rations had been justified. They had planned on having enough to last out a week or more before feeling the pangs of hunger too severely, but the reality fell far short of this. Impudently they decided on a burglary of the British food store. The only trouble was that it might entail a lot of noise. A word with the theatrical group settled that. At a pre-arranged time they launched into a particularly rowdy scene which evinced loud applause, and it was then that the raiding party threw out some packing cases from the store. They got away with much tinned food as well as bread, butter and marmalade, and shared it out with their comrades back in the escape hut.

There were other diversions, and one of the guards, Fred Allsop, remembers the camp as being unusually noisy that night with a lot of singing in the huts close to the wire. In one of them there was even an accordionist in full swing, and when a prisoner opened a window and peeped out Fred shouted jauntily: 'Musica prima!', playing the linguist spiritedly if not accurately. 'Ja, ja,' replied the puzzled German, slamming the window shut. What he told his mates is open to speculation.

In the escape hut itself, however, all was still. The men who gathered there at their appointed times were much too tense and nervous to make a sound. A strict time-table had been worked out so that each escape group knew exactly when they must turn up at Hut 9 to make their way through the tunnel. As each man awaited his turn to lower himself into the shaft, they could hardly believe that their long weeks of toil had come to an end. With their blackened faces they looked strange to one another, and some had attacks of nerves they sought to conceal from their comrades. It still seemed incredible that they had managed to get this far without being discovered, and now their thoughts turned uneasily on what might happen once they were out of the camp and at large in a hostile country. For all they knew, they might be shot like dogs at the first opportunity. Finally, however, they were sustained not only by the fear of appearing cowardly to their friends, but by the faith which their fellow countrymen had in them. At eight o'clock, after their evening meal together, there had been a touching scene in which the comrades they were leaving had come up with messages to be passed on to their families in Germany. They gave them addresses and telephone numbers of wives and parents, pleading with the men who were leaving to contact them as soon as possible. Some took the messages uneasily, privately doubting whether they would get anywhere near the Fatherland, but Hans Harzheim and Werner Zielasko had high hopes of being there in only a day or so. Their plan was to steal an aircraft and fly it back to Germany, dipping its wings over their homeland to convey the message that they were non-combatants.

The plan had been worked out in detail and involved the forging of papers, for they were posing as Norwegian engineers making their way to Croydon Airport. They realized that the papers would not stand close scrutiny, but at a glance they were convincing. They were stamped with an official-looking crown which they had obtained, ironically, from one of the British officers' uniforms which were issued to those

German officers who arrived in Bridgend with no greatcoat at all – and at this stage of the war, with the swift Allied advance through Europe, there were many without greatcoats. These uniforms had a round patch sewn on the back to show that the men wearing them were prisoners of war, but the original buttons were left on them. Harzheim and Zielasko, with the Luftwaffe pilot and U-boat commander who were the other members of their group, used one as a stamp to give their forged papers a superficial look of authenticity. Harzheim, an anti-tank officer, spoke English reasonably well but with a strong accent which they hoped would pass for that of a Norwegian. Harzheim was in a sense their front man, and he had already reconnoitred the immediate area by changing places with one of the other ranks in the working parties. These parties marched daily from the camp under armed escort to load coal at the railway sidings in the middle of Bridgend, and with the collusion of the German sergeant Harzheim donned the uniform and assumed the identity of one of the soldiers on several occasions. His comrades from the lower ranks hid their grins, and with Harzheim swinging his shovel with the best of them, the guards didn't suspect a thing. These unofficial excursions enabled him to obtain a good idea of the geography of the town, and he particularly noticed a car regularly parked overnight outside one of the large Victorian houses in Merthyr Mawr Road, a residential area occupied by professional people. This car came to play a vital part in their plan, for they decided to steal it with the aid of a bunch of ignition keys ingeniously made out of nails. Another useful piece of information which Harzheim carried back to the camp was that there were lorries at a nearby farm from which they could siphon petrol to augment the supply in the tank of the car.

It was shortly after ten o'clock when, as the third escape group, Hans Harzheim and his three comrades crept through the tunnel into the field beyond the wire. Once outside the camp they made straight for Merthyr Mawr Road, where the car was parked as usual. They didn't know it at the time, but it belonged to a general practitioner, Dr R. Baird Milne. Harzheim and the U-boat commander, Oswald Prior, tinkered with the lock while Zielasko and the Luftwaffe pilot, Lieutenant Steffi Ehlert, hurried to the nearby farm just outside the town to siphon some petrol from the lorries. The door opened without much difficulty, but when Harzheim tried to start the car he found to his dismay that the battery was flat. A push start was the obvious answer, but with only one to push that wasn't going to be easy. Just then – and providentially, if one accepts that Providence has a compassionate eye for escaping prisoners of war – four of the guards from Island Farm rolled up on their way back to camp. They were at least one over the eight, and when Harzheim boldly asked them to give a hand they willingly bent to the task without asking any questions. With the Germans inside and the guards pushing for all they were worth the engine picked up at last and the car was on its way, the unsuspecting soldiers standing in the middle of the road jubilantly waving goodbye. A neighbour, looking through the window, assumed that the doctor had been called out urgently and was relieved to see he had received help in starting his car.

Harzheim and Prior picked up their two comrades – who hadn't much luck to report from their siphoning expedition because petrol was desperately short in Britain at that time – and the four men headed for Cardiff along the A48. It was the start of one of the most extraordinary adventures to come out of the escape from Camp 198.

Fortunately for their peace of mind, they did not know that just about the time they were bamboozling the drunken guards, an escaping prisoner had been spotted from a passing taxi. The passengers were Mrs Beatrice Jury and her friend Mrs Deardon, who had come down from Sheffield to spend the week-end with her in Merthyr Mawr. The two ladies decided to give themselves a treat and went to the Embassy Cinema at Bridgend, booking a taxi to take them home – for there were no buses between Bridgend and Merthyr Mawr, and no women in their right minds would wish to walk over two miles home at night past the POW camp.

The taxi was just about to cross the humpback bridge in the narrow country lane leading into Merthyr Mawr village when Mrs Jury looked through the window and saw a man crouching against the low wall at the roadside. In a flash she took in the fact that he was an

Island Farm POW, for she had seen too many of them not to recognize instantly the significance of his clothing.

'Look,' she cried, 'there's a Jerry!'

The driver said something she does not care to repeat.

'But aren't you going to stop?'

'I'm not stopping for no bloody Germans,' he said. 'I'm taking you two ladies home and then I'm going home myself.'

It was half past ten at night, and another four hours were to pass before the general alarm was raised of a mass escape from Island Farm.

'When I found out about it next day,' says Mrs Jury, 'it gave me an awful feeling.' But she insists that, before leaving them, the taxi driver had promised to report the incident. It is tempting to regard his apparent failure to do so as something of overriding importance, yet one must see it in the context of the rest of the events of that night. The escapers had another slice of good fortune when farmer Johnny Davies saw some of them in a field adjoining the camp, but didn't realize it at the time. 'There were these three or four shapes in a ditch,' he said. 'I thought they were dogs.' Understandably, perhaps, but it is hard to account for the authorities' failure to take adequate action in the face of a clear warning from within the compound itself that something was up.

When the escape was actually under way, a middle-aged German officer shambled furtively up to the wire and mumbled a few words to a guard before hurrying away. The startled guard took the message to the duty officer, who did nothing about it until one of his seniors returned from the Conservative club in Bridgend an hour later. The gist of the message was that something was afoot in a hut close to the wire, and although it is not clear if the actual escape hut was identified the general area of activity was. A sergeant and a couple of privates were turfed out to help in what appears to have been a rather cursory investigation, for there was not one man among them who did not feel he was wasting his time. The search party clumped across the now silent camp (the play in the theatre had long ended and so had the impromptu singing) to the vicinity of Hut 9, where they stayed awhile and then went away without entering any of the Germans' quarters. After all, a count of heads at night was a thundering nuisance.

Thus for several hours the escape continued uninterrupted. The ace in the Germans' pack was the electric light in the tunnel, for it served not only to light the way but as a signal. They had look-outs posted on either side of the hut to keep a wary eye on the guard who was patrolling that section of the wire, and when he approached the tunnel exit the light was switched off to warn the men below to lie doggo. When it came on again, they knew it was safe to climb out of the hole. Once through, they made their way along the newly ploughed furrows in the field beyond the wire (first crawling, then stooping and finally running) to a tall

54

tree 150 yards away which they had marked out as a rendezvous. Here the members of each escape group made contact with each other, exhilarated by their success yet restraining their excitement for fear of making a sound that would alert the guards.

There was no moon that night. They had timed their escape well. Everything, it seemed, was on their side.

FIVE

By 2.15am, sixty-five men had escaped from Camp 198. The sixty-sixth to go into the tunnel was Hermann Schallenberg, a Luftwaffe officer, and as he crawled along he heard the sixty-seventh scuffling behind him on his hands and knees. The light went out and he stiffened, as if pulled up short by an invisible string. Hunched up in the darkness, listening to the thumping of his own heart and breathing the foul air, he had a sense of unreality. It seemed incredible that this time, he would actually crawl through that hole at the end of the tunnel.

The light went on again and the scuffling procession resumed. The gradient steepened and suddenly there was the hole just ahead. Hermann pushed his way through and the clean night air filled his lungs. He remembered the way the Welsh farmer had looked, swinging his tractor round, just missing the stone they had put there to cover the hole.

As he crawled across the ploughed field, his hands and knees sank into the soft earth of the furrow. Even the smallest sounds seemed, to his taut nerves, capable of betraying their presence to the guards. He thought about the dogs and wondered that they had not caught the scent of so many men. In a small space of time he thought about many things.

Then came a shout, followed by a shot and a cry of pain. The guard came running, blowing his whistle. The man just behind him was moaning softly and he wondered how badly he was hurt, but there was no way of finding out without running the risk of being shot himself and giving all the others away into the bargain. He lay prone as the camp came suddenly to life with the shouting of guards and the barking of dogs. Could they possibly escape now? The guards clustered round the wounded man, so close to Hermann Schallenberg that he feared they must trip over him. Their loud, excited voices jabbered on, and still there was nothing to do but lie there. He could hear the soldiers ferreting around the perimeter bank, trying to discover how the prisoner had managed to reach the other side of the wire. Suddenly there was a yell, followed by a string of all the best curses a Tommy could muster.

Hermann realized at once what had happened. The guard had fallen into their escape hole. It was too much for him. He laughed.

'Stand up, you bastard!'

Hermann clambered to his feet, hands held high. His comrades were laughing as well. The guards didn't appreciate the joke.

'Christ almighty!' cried one of them. 'Look at this lot! Half the German bloody army's here!'

Ten men in the field were surrendering with broad grins.

'Jesus Christ,' moaned a guard. 'Now we're for the fucking high jump.'

At Bridgend police station, the young constable flung open the door and shouted, 'Sergeant, sergeant, something terrible's happened! The prisoners have escaped from Island Farm!'

Sergeant Bill Jones, wbo had been on his way to the railway station for the regular routine of meeting the night mail, ran back up the hill.

'The commandant's on the line now, Sarge.'

The sergeant spoke to Lieutenant-Colonel Darling. 'I can't be sure yet, but I think they're all accounted for,' said the commandant confidently. 'A guard shot one fellow in the shoulder outside the wire and we nabbed another ten. We're making a count now.'

Within a few minutes, Superintendent May and Inspector Fitzpatrick had been roused from their beds and were on their way to Island Farm. They found the place in an uproar, with prisoners jeering the harassed guards and in an air of jubilation they had never seen before. Darling, trying as best he could to maintain a commanding presence, assured them that this little plot had been nipped in the bud.

'Can you account for all your prisoners, Colonel?' asked May when the count was over.

'Every one of them,' said Darling.

'Are you sure now?'

'Quite sure.'

He explained that the prisoners had been checked off in pairs as they passed through the gate between one compound and another. It had been the devil's own job getting some of the blighters out of bed, but at last they

58

had managed it and the numbers were right. The wounded prisoner had been taken to Bridgend hospital, and the other ten were in the guardroom. A full investigation would be held.

'Don't you worry, gentlemen,' repeated the tall, willowy Darling, his self-confidence blooming again like a rose in high summer, 'they're all accounted for all right. We'll get to the bottom of this little plot, and make sure the same thing doesn't happen again.'

Britons to the core, they all sat down and drank strong cups of tea. By now the tunnel had been traced back to Hut 9, but since the only eleven men to have used it were safely back in the fold there seemed little point in staying on to bandy pleasantries in the small hours of the morning. May and Fitzpatrick glanced at each other, finished their tea and duly said their farewells.

'I'll give you a ring in the morning,' said May, 'to make sure everything's all right.'

'Don't you worry about that, Superintendent,' said Darling with a smile. 'It's all perfectly in order. These things are sent to try us, what?'

The two police officers walked back to their car. 'Nice start to a Sunday,' said Fitzpatrick with a smile.

'Well,' said May gravely, 'it could have been a lot worse. If there really *had* been a mass escape . . .'

'Just think how many could have gone through that tunnel.'

'That's just what I *am* thinking,'

'Mr May, sir!'

The cry from behind made them stop and turn. It was a soldier with a message for the Superintendent.

'There's a call for you, sir. One of your men at the police station is on the line. Would you take it in the orderly room?'

It was the duty sergeant reporting that PC Baverstock, of Llanharan, had captured two German officers and was keeping them in custody at the village police station, eight miles from Bridgend.

'Ask Baverstock what time they got out,' said May grimly.

'I have, sir. They said they were out at ten o'clock and that they were the seventh and eighth men through the tunnel.'

May put down the phone and broke the news to Darling.

One of the two men in custody at Llanharan was Lieutenant Karl Ludwig, the SS officer who still had hopes of a revival in Germany's fortunes. Powerfully built, and over six feet tall, his months in captivity had not robbed him of the audaciousness that typified the men of the Waffen-SS on the battlefield. He and his friend Heinz Herzler had hit on the idea of jumping aboard one of the American trucks that passed Island Farm every night on their way to Cardiff docks and thence to the Continent. They would hide in the truck, steal a free passage to France by courtesy of the Allies and sneak out when the coast was clear. 'I had a lot of French friends,' Karl Ludwig explains. 'I knew that one of them would take me in and maybe I'd do a bit of work on the farm to earn my keep.' And then? 'Then,' he says, 'I would wait for the German army to come back to France.'

It was Ludwig's bad luck that the night they chose to escape there were no American trucks passing the camp. As he and Herzler stood by a traffic light, however, a car pulled up at the red and it struck Ludwig that they could do worse than hitch a lift and bluff it out – for of course, the escape had not yet been discovered. When he glanced inside, he changed his mind – for with four people already in the Austin, there was clearly no room for any more. It was only when he was back in captivity that he found that this had been Dr Milne's car, and that the occupants were none other than his old comrades Harzheim, Zielasko, Prior and Ehlert.

After waiting in vain for a lorry to turn up, they decided to try their luck at the railway station. As they walked through the darkened streets of Bridgend, however, they came up against a new problem: a man returning home worse for wear after a night on the beer. They hopped over a garden wall and the man came in through the gate just as his wife opened the door and started yelling at him. He shouted back, she slammed the door and the reveller made his own special comment on the state of matrimony by urinating where he stood. Unfortunately, Karl Ludwig happened to be in his direct line of fire. Lying on the ground practically under the feet of the enemy, he took it like a man. His assailant went indoors, unaware that he had done something to an

SS officer that many people would have given ten years of their lives to do. Ludwig rose to his feet and shook off the indignity. Herzler nearly collapsed with laughter.

Reaching the station they crept on to a goods wagon, but the train's progress was painfully slow and, although they weren't to know it, it was moving in the wrong direction. When it stopped at a little marshalling yard they jumped off and tried to get their bearings. It was no use: they were lost. Well, there was only one thing for it and that was to move on and hope to hit the road to Cardiff. Before they had gone far from the station, however, it was their misfortune to encounter PC Philip Baverstock on patrol on his bicycle. He saw them lurking by the roadside and took them for burglars.

'Who are you?' said Baverstock sternly, shining his torch on them.

'And who are you?' replied Ludwig impudently.

'I think you'd better come along with me.'

'But why? I'm only a poor Welsh miner out looking for food for my children!'

'A likely story,' said the policeman, reflecting that something strange must have happened overnight in the Valleys if Welsh miners were suddenly sporting Teutonic accents. Pushing his bike, he walked beside them and wondered if they might make a break for it. So they would have, if Ludwig hadn't been uncomfortably aware of an ominous bulge under the policeman's long coat. He thought it was a gun, whereas it was only a truncheon. 'If I'd known he didn't have a gun,' laments an older and wiser Karl Ludwig today, 'I'd have taken his bike!'

In the police station PC Baverstock switched on the light and took a good look at his suspects. They were both six-footers, with a military bearing even in captivity. They were wearing capes and beneath them were their army uniforms. He rang Bridgend to report the capture of two German prisoners of war.

Now the game was up, Ludwig and Herzler weren't in a mood to make trouble. There was a philosophical streak in them and besides, they were rather taken by the polite, formal manners of this village policeman. They allowed him to search their haversacks and he found them well stocked with corned beef, ersatz coffee and other edibles, and cocoa tins packed with cigarettes. They had even found room for their slippers and shaving kits!

'Meant to make yourselves comfortable, didn't you?' he said with a smile.

'Why not?' was the bland reply. 'It isn't every day you break out of prison!'

What intrigued Baverstock most, however, was the tail of a shirt. On it was a map, drawn with painstaking accuracy, showing the main railway lines and ports in southern England and northern France.

A more meticulous count had taken place at Island Farm and this revealed that sixty-seven men had passed through the tunnel, including the eleven recaptured just outside the wire. An escape of this size was scarcely imaginable, but Superintendent May wasn't the sort of man to indulge in futile brooding. He knew they had to move fast, for with a four or five-hour start some of the Germans could already be well on their way to quitting the country. The wires were hot as police stations and military bases were alerted, and as dawn broke on that Sunday morning policemen – including specials and war reserves – and military personnel were dragged from their beds to mount a manhunt which, in its scale and organization, had few precedents in Britain. In Bill May's words, 'the sky was the limit', and he was uncomfortably aware of his own warning that 'the escaping prisoner has opportunities for sabotage in abundance in this division'. Neither he nor anyone else knew at this stage the motives for the escape: it could be part of a sinister plot to disrupt vital installations, a plot involving spies and quislings. Indeed, the clever way it had been engineered, and the number of men involved, suggested this as a distinct possibility. But in any event, the thought of fifty-six tough young Nazis roaming the countryside – thirsting for revenge, perhaps, for the beating their country was taking at the hands of the Allies – was enough of a worry in itself. There was no knowing how they would react to freedom, nor how people would react to them.

Some of the earliest calls went out to signalmen who, in their high, lonely boxes in out-of-the-way places, played a vital role in the running of a railway system far less automated than today's. They could be relied on to keep a sharp look-out for strangers, and since they were

64

by nature self-sufficient men they would keep a cool head in a crisis. Denis Skyrme, who was on duty at Pencoed West signal box a few miles from Bridgend, remembers receiving a call from the train controller in Cardiff telling all signalmen of the escape. 'We were told to advise drivers and guards and to watch no one hopped aboard if they stopped at the signals,' he said. A goods train plying between Cardiff and Llanelli was stopped at Bridgend in the small hours of the morning and police and railwaymen examined every wagon, as well as poking into possible hiding places in the goods yard. After being told the men might be dangerous, the engine driver took the precaution of arming himself with a brake stick, and when at last he was allowed to resume the journey he noticed that every time they passed a signal box the man inside would lean out and flash a torch on the wagons.

Superintendent May set up an operations room at Bridgend police station, with a large-scale map on the wall and an array of little flags bearing swastikas to stick into it whenever a prisoner was recaptured. The plan which until then had existed only on paper was now converted into reality, and those motorists with enough petrol to take to the road were stopped at road blocks and asked to produce their identity cards. May was determined to make everyone feel responsible for doing his or her bit, which apart from its practical benefits would have the psychological advantage of giving the civilian population the sense of being part of a team. The last thing he wanted was panic, and a feeling of isolation in the scattered farms and hamlets. So, in accordance with that circular he had issued nearly three months before, people were asked to immobilize their vehicles when not using them, and to tell the police if they saw anything in the least suspicious.

Meanwhile, the prisoner who had been shot while escaping was in Bridgend hospital. His name was Lieutenant Tönnsmann and, ironically, he had no rightful part in the escape at all. He was, in simple terms, a gatecrasher, and it was his lack of basic preparation that had betrayed his presence to the guard. For Tönnsmann, to his eternal discredit, had been carrying a white kitbag – and this had shown up in the dark.

SIX

Farmers in the Vale of Glamorgan had a puzzling experience when they left their beds early on that Sunday morning and clattered into their cowsheds. They found that, inexplicably, someone had milked the cows before them. It was only when they heard of the mass escape that they realized what had happened. 'The cheeky devils,' they grumbled. 'First they dig a tunnel and then they help themselves to our ruddy milk!'

There were other signs of aliens in their midst as well. Phil Brunsdon, a farmworker on the Merthyr Mawr estate, found on his routine morning round that two of his pitchforks were missing. 'I thought that kids had taken them,' he said. It was, in fact, the strangest Sunday of the war for the villagers of Merthyr Mawr. The local gamekeeper, Arthur Wilkinson, was rudely awakened by shouts from the bamboo thicket at the back of his cottage. 'What the dickens is going on out there?' he said wonderingly to his wife. He looked out of the window and saw armed soldiers stumping around in the undergrowth. 'We're looking for Jerries,' they shouted back at him when he demanded an explanation.

The first sign that some of the Germans who had taken part in the escape were less enthusiastic about it than others came when William Board was milking at

Home Farm, Merthyr Mawr, just before 7am. 'I heard the latch go and looked up and saw four of them standing there watching me,' he said. This, to say the least, was a surprise, since at the time he didn't know there were any out of the camp. He went to the door and they walked past him, whispering among themselves, and stood against the wall. 'It was then I saw the soldiers,' said Mr Board. 'They were coming from the orchard with their rifles and searching the barns. When they came closer they shouted: "Have you seen any Germans round here?" I told them they were standing just behind me and in they came. But you should have seen the way they stuck their bayonets in the hay to make sure there weren't any more around the farm! I think those Germans came into the milking shed because they felt safer in with me than out in the open with those soldiers on the warpath!'

William Board has an interesting theory that the men might have made a successful run for it if they had known that the River Ewenny flowed into the River Ogmore just south of the village. Making straight for the sea after leaving the camp, they had found themselves caught in a trap at the confluence of the rivers because the tide was in. 'They had to double back into the village but by that time the soldiers were looking for them,' he said.

They weren't the only Germans who went south, however, for a driver with the Welsh Regiment, Joseph Haworth, had spotted two of them in a field while haring towards the sand dunes in his truck. He was stationed at Maindy Barracks in Cardiff and was woken up by a policeman at 5.30am to take an officer back to Island Farm as soon as possible. The officer, Captain Rees, was one of the camp personnel but had spent the night at Maindy. When they reached the camp, Rees told him to make for the shore to see if there were signs of any craft waiting to take the Germans away. 'Just before I reached the dunes,' said Joe, who played county cricket for Lancashire before the war, 'I saw these two Germans in a field in the distance. They were crawling along raising their bodies now and then to look around. I didn't stop because my orders were to get down to the sea as soon as possible. I walked over the dunes but there was no sign of any ship.'

Later that Sunday, Captain Rees trudged over the dunes on his own to look for signs of a vessel. The theory was that there could be one lurking in the Bristol Channel to take the prisoners to Ireland, which flattered them with a degree of organization they did not possess. At the very least, however, the authorities knew that those sand dunes between Merthyr Mawr and the sea afforded the escaped prisoners an ideal hiding place for men on the run. There were three or four square miles of dunes, a small desert of sand and marram grass sweeping up to heights of over one hundred feet and hiding remains of Iron Age settlements. 'We searched the sandhills at Merthyr Mawr for two days,' said Glyn McNeil, a young constable at the time who became landlord of the 'Horse and Groom' in Cowbridge. 'We looked in old dugouts, little caves, that sort of thing. We were exhausted.' Even in normal times, a policeman's life was hard graft in 1945. 'Our normal shift was 6am to 6pm,' he recalled, 'with one day off a week if you were lucky.'

One of the keenest searchers was Jack Jones, the Merthyr Mawr rat-catcher, who despite his rheumaticky legs dragged himself over the dunes to join in the hunt. When he saw some soldiers engaged in what seemed a futile exercise, he urged them to do something more positive about finding the Germans. 'Don't come bothering us about Germans,' snapped the young officer in charge. 'We're training to fight the Japs!' It was this attitude, perhaps, that enabled two of the escapers to evade capture for several days by hiding in a cave near the ruins of Candleston Castle, now a favourite picnic spot on the fringe of the dunes. Searchers came across the smouldering remains of wood fires, with fresh peelings of carrots and turnips scattered around, but by that time the Germans – realizing, perhaps, that their den was no longer secret – had moved on.

Two miles to the west a party of Girl Guides unexpectedly came up against the enemy while in Danygraig Wood at Newton, just outside the seaside resort of Porthcawl. By this time it was late afternoon and the mist was rolling in from the sea. It was all jolly good fun, with sausages sizzling in the frying pan over the camp fire, and some of the girls wandered away from the rest to do a bit of exploring on their own. Suddenly two figures appeared out of the gloom and said, 'Is this the way to Porthcawl?' The girls were startled, for the men spoke in strange accents, and after murmuring a reply they ran back and told Miss Olive Nicholl, who was in charge of the party. 'It must be two of the escaped prisoners!' she cried, much to the delight of the intrepid Guides.

'They were very excited,' Miss Nicholl recalls. 'The girls all wanted to set out in search of the Germans, but I told them the best thing they could do was to go into Porthcawl and tell the *South Wales Echo* man what had happened. So off they went and when I got home I rang up various people and we searched Danygraig Wood. It was dark by then and we all set off with lanterns. You must remember that the men were away fighting. We women thought it was up to us to do something. Life was so sad and miserable, with food short and people being killed, then suddenly out of the blue came this bit of excitement!' The drama had an unforeseen result, for at the next Guide meeting fifteen new recruits turned up in the hope of more thrills in the future.

It wasn't only on the coast that visibility was poor. Bill Jones, the police sergeant who had taken the call from the commandant the previous night, remembers that fog had hampered the search inland for the first day or two. His first job was to go to Wern Tarw Colliery, seven miles from the camp between Pencoed and Heol-y-cyw, where there was a coke oven which had been made by German engineers just before the war. In fact, they had still been working on it at the outbreak of war, when they were interned – somewhat ungraciously, one feels, if necessarily. That nagging fear of sabotage prompted the thought that the Germans on the run might be out to destroy the installations into which their compatriots had put so much effort, so Sergeant Jones led a search and posted a guard before pressing on to his second objective – the mountainous country between Llanharan and Gilfach Goch. These bleak uplands, rising to close on 1,000 feet in height and gloomily crowned by a tumulus, would have daunted the bravest of spirits, but it was the sergeant's task to establish that no Germans had chosen it as their escape route. He could be pardoned for thinking that simpler duties than this had been rewarded with medals. Putting a bold face on it, he rallied his team and set out along the mountain tracks, paying special attention to the outbuildings of lonely farms and the forlorn ruins of cottages and long-deserted churches. His keen sense of history reminded him that when the conquering Normans had come nine centuries ago, they had stayed south of this physical barrier, and he felt ready to admire their good sense and preference for easy pickings.

Back at Bridgend, the police station was throbbing with more activity than it had ever known before. As the first flags were pinned to the wall map denoting the capture of the four prisoners at Home Farm, Sergeant Percy Green was on the phone to the camp adjutant taking a list of the names and descriptions of the men still at large. He immediately rang around the police stations to pass on the information, feeling that speed was of the essence in an operation of this kind. When the Chief Constable looked in, however, he took a different view, and criticized him for not sending out the descriptions in the form of a circular.

In his anxiety to spread the word as quickly as possible, Superintendent May was ready to employ unorthodox methods. There were no town criers in the Vale of Glamorgan any more, but there were men of the cloth with captive audiences in churches and chapels – and then, Sunday worship was an integral part of life in that community. May knew that an announcement from the pulpit would be the best way of getting his message across, and his request to this effect was conveyed to as many clergy as possible. They agreed to help, but the doctrine they had to impart was capable of as many interpretations as the faith itself. Some emphasized the need to love one's enemies, even while being wary of their actions, while others gave their anxious flocks the impression that they were encompassed by the troops of Midian.

It was at Laleston, two miles west of Island Farm along the A48, that the most dramatic method of warning the population was employed. The church bells were rung for the first time since Winston Churchill had ruled in 1940 that they were to be used henceforth only as a warning that Britain had been invaded.

Predictably, Dad's Army didn't wait to be invited to hunt the *Herrenvolk*. Although, with the threat of a Nazi invasion just a bad memory, the Home Guard had been officially stood down, its members now volunteered to join the search as eagerly as they had stepped into the ranks at the outbreak of war. Jack Struel, a Bridgend draper who had served not only in the Home Guard but in the Local Defence Volunteers that preceded it, took three policemen who were stuck for transport on the first day of the search to Pencoed in his own car. When they stopped for petrol the garage proprietor, capturing the spirit of the occasion, filled up his tank without asking for money or petrol coupons – and just as they were pulling away he called them to a halt and thrust some packets of sweets through the window. 'You'll need something to chew,' he said. 'You could have a long day ahead of you!' What gave this gesture a special meaning is that sweets were on ration too.

The sector commander of the Home Guard was Colonel William Llewellyn, who found the grounds of his large country house, Court Colman, being searched by policemen and soldiers. As a good patriot he didn't object, but thought it all rather a waste of time. 'I could have told them there weren't any escaped Germans there because my gamekeepers used to go around the covers first thing in the morning, and they could tell from the dew whether anything had happened overnight. They could read the signs, y'know – and what's more they were in the Home Guard too!'

The escape came too late to make the Sunday papers, but the BBC reported it in their radio bulletins in the deadpan style which would have made even the announcement of Armageddon sound like a routine occasion. It is important not to underestimate the effect the news had on people in the more isolated areas. Women locked their doors and lived for days in fear of the lurking Fascist beast. 'We didn't know what to expect at first,' recalled Special Constable Ernest Nott, long after the event. 'The Germans could have been armed for all we knew. We were told not to go too near them if we were on our own, and to shout at them asking if they spoke English. We weren't given firearms, just a pair of handcuffs and a truncheon, and we used to go out searching the fields and hedges. I remember going out once with an American officer. He had a big revolver and said he was "gonna kill the bastards". He would have, too!'

As Sunday dinner went uneaten in many households and the afternoon snooze was forgotten, Observer Corps posts were being manned and the guard strengthened at ordnance factories and military bases. Leave was cancelled for servicemen, who scoured the countryside in a fashion which, in retrospect, seems peculiarly British. 'I was stationed at the command workshops at Litchard Cross, not far from Bridgend,' said Ken Jenkins, who was a REME craftsman. 'It was a normal sort of Sunday, a bit on the quiet side, when suddenly we were all paraded back to the works and informed that a lot of prisoners had escaped from Island Farm. After considerable messing about two troop-carrying vehicles were brought to the unit and we were all shipped aboard, about thirty or forty of us, and taken to Llantrisant. When we got there we were told we'd have different areas to patrol but we didn't know at first that we'd only have push-bikes! Out came the bikes and the orders were to scour the countryside for the prisoners. Mind, there was a lot of countryside between Llantrisant and Cardiff and to tell you the truth, we weren't really bothered whether the Jerries got away or not. My pal Eric looked at me and said, "Well, we're going home for supper now, Ken." Because he was a Cardiff lad like myself. So off we went and cycled ten miles home and had a beautiful supper.'

They met up at four o'clock next morning after a good night's sleep and began to cycle slowly back to Litchard Cross, feeling rather pleased with the Germans for presenting them with such an agreeable break in routine. Just outside Cardiff, however, in the village of St Fagans, they found the local bobby on patrol. They were ready for a friendly chat, but he wasn't.

'I want proof of your identity,' he said suspiciously.

'But we're in the army!' they protested. 'We've been out searching for the escaped prisoners from Island Farm.'

'You could be two of them for all I know. Give me proof of your identity.'

'Oh, come on! Where d'you think we got these uniforms?'

'That's just what I'd like to know. You could have clobbered a British soldier and taken his uniform or anything. And anyway,' said the policeman, struck by a flash of inspiration, 'if you're out looking for Germans, what d'you think you're going to catch them with? You've got no arms, have you?'

'That's not our fault, is it? We weren't even given a stick to hold, leave alone guns!'

'So how were you supposed to capture them?'

'Well,' said Ken, and the story was so improbable that the constable just had to believe it, 'we were told that if we came up against a German, one of us could keep him talking while the other went for help.'

It wasn't the kind of thing the GIs were used to, as Eddie Bailey recalls all too well. He was a bus driver with Cardiff Corporation, and one of his tasks was to ferry busloads of Americans to a military hospital at Rhydlafar, eight miles away. When the search for the Germans was in full swing, he was stopped by a policeman at Radyr Chain, a crossroads just outside the city boundary, and told that a farm labourer had seen one of them go through a wire fence into a field.

'I can do with some help. Care to give me a hand?'

'I don't mind,' said Eddie. 'I'm a special myself, anyway' – meaning a special constable.

'Think this lot would help as well?' asked the policeman, casting his eyes round the bus.

'Why not?' said Eddie. 'They're on our side, aren't they?' But a few seconds later, he wasn't so sure.

'They wouldn't budge. They just sat tight in their seats,' he says today, looking back with a mixture of amazement and disgust. 'They said they weren't prepared to go because they weren't armed. "He isn't armed either," I said to them. "He's a prisoner." But no, they wouldn't move. It took me at least a quarter of an hour to get four of them to come with me, and then it was only because they were shamed into it by the fact that there were women on the bus. And the joke of it is, I'm only a little chap and they were great hefty blokes, but I was the mug leading them and they were trailing behind. We got three parts of the way round the field and they wouldn't go any further.'

SEVEN

After conning the drunken guards into starting the car
for them, Hans Harzheim and his three companions
headed for Cardiff along the A48. They had a long way
to go because they were making for Croydon, where
they knew there was a large airport. It quickly became
clear, however, that the actual taking of an aircraft
might turn out to be child's play compared with the task
of steering the right course for Croydon. Wartime
Britain could be a nightmare for the traveller uncertain
of his route and, after dark, zealous ARP wardens
patrolled the streets ready to pounce on anyone who
dared to show an unauthorized chink of light. It's true
that by this time the blackout had been modified into
something known as the dim-out, but even so street
lighting was poor and in addition there was the vexing
problem for Harzheim of steering on the left-hand side
of the road. This was the first time he had driven a car
in Britain and for a while he faced a chorus of 'Left,
Hans, left!' from his passengers. It was after midnight
when they drove down Tumble Hill, with its hazardous
bend at the bottom, and past the council houses of Ely
at the western approaches of Cardiff. This was the way
that in happier times coachloads of fans came,
festooned with rosettes, on their way to rugby

internationals at the Arms Park, but it would have taken a strong imagination to conjure up even the ghost of a cheer on that cold March night. The lights were still out all over Europe, and Harzheim, Zielasko, Ehlert and Prior had the streets to themselves as they rattled along in their 'borrowed' Austin 10 into the heart of the city.

Suddenly they saw two policemen standing on a street corner staring at them, and Harzheim instinctively took the next turning to get out of their view. To his horror he found it was a dead end, and he had to turn the car around and go back the same way. By this time he had recovered his nerve and he gave the bobbies a bold glance as he drove past them, reminding himself that since they were wearing civilian clothes over their uniforms (clothes bought with cigarettes from the German railway officials interned as POWs at Island Farm) there was nothing obviously suspicious in their appearance. All they had to do now was put the city behind them as quickly as possible, but that was easier said than done. The unfamiliar streets baffled them, and when they found themselves back in the same place they had been ten minutes before, they had to admit the awful truth: they were lost.

'Hans. Look. Over there.'

It was a lonely figure trudging along the pavement. Someone going home, perhaps, to a wife, a family. A stranger. A friendly stranger?

'Let's ask him the way.'

They stopped the car and smiled, four amiable Norwegians sure of the help of a trusty British ally.

'Excuse me, please.'

To their own ears, their accents sounded grotesque and patently Germanic. But the man beamed back.

'It's the Newport road you want, boys. I'm going that way myself. Can I hop in?'

They made room for him in the back seat and he squeezed in.

'Off to Croydon then, are you? That's a fair old journey. Can't say I'd fancy it myself at this time of night. What time you expecting to get there?'

They answered him politely, trying not to sound evasive, sticking to their prepared story.

'Engineers, eh? Damn sight more interesting than my job!'

He was a tram driver going home after a late-night shift. On the outskirts of Cardiff he took his leave of them.

'Remember the way now? Straight on for Newport, and after that it's the Gloucester road you want.' He clambered out. 'Good luck!'

But they needed more luck than was coming their way because they ran out of petrol between Chepstow and Gloucester and had to abandon the car in a field near Two Bridges, just outside Blakeney, after trying unsuccessfully to break into a garage. In the dawn light they took stock. They had travelled eighty miles but were not even half-way to Croydon. They fought back depression, born of fatigue and a sense of anti-climax.

'What do we do now?'

'Hide. That's the first thing. They're sure to be looking for us soon.'

'I wonder if they've found the tunnel yet?'

'It'll be a miracle if they haven't.'

'Well, it's a miracle they didn't find it before we even finished it.'

'That's true.'

'The time the commandant stood on top of it without noticing anything!'

They shared a laugh and the tension eased.

'Come on, let's get going.'

They made for a thicket in the middle of a big field, thinking they would be safe in there till nightfall. But a herd of inquisitive cows insisted on following them and staring at them with their large, liquid eyes.

'Go away! Shoo!'

The cows remained.

'It's no good. Those stupid cows will give us away!'

The Germans crept out of hiding, but were spotted by some farm workers. Alarmed by their shouts, they ran into the nearby forest. Later that morning, as they ate sparingly of their rations and took it in turns to doze off, they heard the sound of aircraft overhead.

'I wonder if they're looking for us?'

They were. The hunt was on and, before the day was out, scores of soldiers with rifles and tommy-guns were searching the Forest of Dean, with gamekeepers and foresters acting as guides. The rumours started flying and, that night in Fleet Street, a *Daily Mirror* sub-editor hit on a snappy but inaccurate headline: 'Planes and troops hunt armed Nazi prisoners'. For the nearest thing to a weapon possessed by the fugitives was the bunch of makeshift keys with which they had snaffled the car that had served them well, but not quite well enough.

Back in Bridgend, the schoolboys were having a field day. Armed with sticks and catapults, the braver spirits among them sallied out to join in the hunt. Some were sent packing by irate soldiers who had enough trouble on their hands without packs of kids yelping at their heels, but others found themselves involved in extraordinary adventures they remember vividly to this day.

Gwyn Leyshon, a sturdy nine-year-old who became building manager of a firm of civil engineers in Port Talbot, was one of them. He lived in the village of Pencoed, five miles from Island Farm, and on that Sunday morning he and his pals were out and about early, excited by the breakfast-time talk of a mass-escape by the Germans. They wandered across the fields, not really expecting to find any Jerries – and, in their heart of hearts, rather hoping they wouldn't. They made for Coedymwstwr Woods, one of their favourite haunts, where there were secret hollows thickly carpeted with bluebells and gnarled old oaks they could climb as easily as squirrels. They were still on the edge of the woods, however, when Gwyn saw an old pair of boots in the bracken. Useful, he thought – just the thing for playing soldiers, even if they were a bit on the large side. He stretched out a hand to take them, then sprang back with a cry when a man who seemed ten feet tall to his astonished eyes jumped up from the undergrowth.

Those 'abandoned' boots had contained a pair of feet – German feet. Their owner turned tail with his companion, who had emerged from the bracken a few feet away, and the two men ran uphill through the woods without a word. 'Jerries!' thought the lads, and ran helter-skelter back to the village, where they knew the army had road blocks. They gabbled their tale to an officer, who promptly sent search parties into the woods, but it was some hours later that the men were caught in Coity, on the other side of the hill.

'Those boots were so old and mangled that I thought someone had just dumped them there,' recalls Gwyn Leyshon, with a sense of relish in his youthful escapade. 'It gave me the shock of my life when those two men jumped up! They were wearing a denim sort of uniform and carrying boxes on their backs like haversacks. They were square boxes which looked as though they'd been made out of odd bits of wood. I suppose they held their rations for the escape.'

The search for Germans didn't go on only at ground level, for as the boys tucked into their Sunday dinners they could hear aircraft buzzing overhead. Light Austers, each carrying a pilot and observer, were sweeping as low as they dared and, hearing them, the men on the run felt that sense of isolation which afflicts even the bravest of the hunted when the hunter is hard on their heels.

At her home in Laleston, Brenda Morris had an idea. 'I think they ought to take a look in School Wood,' she told her father, farmer Elwyn Morris. 'They'd probably find some of the Jerries in that hollow I used to play in when I was a kid. That's where I'd go if I was looking for somewhere to hide, anyway.'

'That's a thought,' said Elwyn quietly. 'I might take a look there myself.'

'You be careful now,' said his wife severely. 'Those Germans could have guns for all you know. You're too old for cowboys and Indians. Leave them to the police and the soldiers.'

But if there were Germans anywhere near his land, Elwyn wanted to know. So did his neighbour, John Williams. The two farmers set out, with stout sticks to protect themselves from the pride of the German army.

Meanwhile, Ivor Jenkins had heard a strange rustling deep in the bushes in School Wood. He was out looking for beansticks, having disregarded some pointed remarks earlier in the day that he ought to be out hunting the prisoners with every other able-bodied patriot. 'Prisoners be damned,' was his reply. 'If the whole of the bloody German army's broken out, I'm going for a walk!' He thought the rustling was being made by cows which had wandered into the woods, and fearing they might strangle themselves in the tangle of twigs and briars, he decided to warn the nearest farmer. First, however, he would have a quiet smoke, for it was peaceful in the woods and Germans or no Germans, the war seemed very far away. He sat down, stretched his legs and lit up. And then his dog started barking.

'Quiet, boy!' said Ivor. 'What's wrong with you?'

The dog kept on barking.

'Rabbits, is it? Where?'

And then Ivor heard voices.

'Ssh! Quiet boy!' commanded Ivor urgently.

The dog settled for some intermittent growls. Ivor made his way to a hedge and looked over it. There were several men sprawled in a clearing, wearing some kind of uniform. One of them saw Ivor and coolly returned his gaze. Ivor hurried to his father's house, across the fields in Llangewydd. 'Are there any forestry boys around here, Dad?' he said.

'No, not to my way of thinking.'

'Well, there's some men in the woods wearing the same kind of clothes.'

'Foresters . . . ? Damn, it can't be them prisoners of war, can it? What are they dressed in?'

Ivor told him.

'You bet that's what they are!' cried his father. 'You go over and tell Ben and Dai and we'll get moving.'

A neighbour was dispatched on a motor-bike to the nearest police station and it wasn't long before a search party of policemen and farmers were on the trail. By this time Elwyn Morris and John Williams were in School Wood themselves, and, creeping up to the hollow which Brenda had described, they saw the men whom, unknown to them, Ivor Jenkins had just spotted. They had obviously been enjoying a picnic, but so far as Elwyn was concerned the party was over. 'You'd better surrender,' he shouted, waving his stick at them. 'We've got you surrounded!'

Some of the Germans looked so uncertain that it seemed for a moment that his bluff might succeed, but at a sharp command from the officer evidently in charge of the group they scrambled through a hedge.

'What do we do now?' cried Elwyn desperately. 'We can't let them get away!'

The sound of a plane gave him the inspiration he needed. He tied his white handkerchief to his stick and, running into the middle of the clearing, waved it frantically as a signal. The observer saw it and the pilot banked and swooped low over the tree tops as the two men gesticulated in the direction the prisoners had taken. The observer gave them the thumbs-up and radioed for help. The farmers wiped their brows. It was hot work chasing Germans.

The search party from Llangewydd, stumping through the woods in single file, knew nothing of this drama. In fact, the police sergeant was a bit dubious that Ivor Jenkins had seen anything suspicious at all.

'I think it's a false alarm,' he said morosely, thinking longingly of the Sunday afternoon snooze he'd be enjoying if the blasted Jerries hadn't taken it into their heads to escape.

'Don't be so dull,' snapped Ivor. 'They're round here somewhere all right.'

So they were, and with the military converging on the woods their taste of freedom was about to end in the bitterness of recapture. Ivor remembers the amount of food they had with them. 'They had everything. Some things we hadn't had for bloody years.' And he remembers what the German who had looked him straight in the eye earlier said as he was led away. 'Bastard,' he mouthed at Ivor, evidently blaming him entirely for their defeat.

When the word went back to search HQ, Superintendent May triumphantly stuck five swastikas in his wall map to add to those already there. He wasn't a man to indulge in false optimism, but the hunt was going well. Already twelve men had been recaptured, in addition to the eleven taken just outside the wire, which left forty-four of the escapers still on the loose. And to his immense relief, so far there had been no reports of violence, or even any threat of it. On the contrary, when cornered the Germans seemed prepared to surrender peacefully. 'They were a cunning lot,' he would say. 'If they knew you were on top, they were very polite. But if they had the whip hand you knew they'd never let you forget it.'

As the hours ticked by on that unforgettable Sunday, there were more successes for the hunters. A woman serving in the women's branch of the army, the ATS, spotted two strange men crossing a field, and striding up to them purposefully cried in an accusing voice, 'You're German prisoners, aren't you?' Perhaps it was their half-hearted attitude to the escape as much as their fear of being shot that persuaded them to surrender without even giving her the satisfaction of a chase, for some of the Germans had joined in the adventure only because they were bullied into it by their more enthusiastic comrades. So much was obvious when the hunt was scarcely under way, for in the early hours of Sunday morning one of the prisoners had had the nerve to tap the door of a terraced house to ask for food. He was in jackboots and a Luftwaffe greatcoat and the terrified woman who answered the door, then in ignorance of the escape and assuming he had been shot down on the mountains, mumbled something and slammed the door in his face. Trembling with fright, she woke her family and soon afterwards the undistinguished escaper was captured by the police.

Surprisingly, in spite of all the excitement some people living only the length of a football pitch from the main gates of the camp knew nothing about the escape until the six o'clock news on the radio that evening. 'We were astonished,' said Mrs Nancy Wragg. 'A friend came round later and asked us if we felt safe, and I said we did – because we knew that once the Germans got out of the camp, they'd be wanting to get as far away from it as possible!'

Next morning, a weary William May was back at his desk early after snatching a few hours' sleep. By now the map was liberally dotted with flags, for late on Sunday evening six more prisoners had been rounded up in a quarry at Kenfig Hill, west of the camp on the way to Swansea. This left thirty-six still at large. As they went to work on that Monday morning, many men left behind them desperately anxious wives or mothers who hated being alone with so many Nazis roaming around. It was common knowledge that the Bridgend

89

camp was full of SS, a term that conjured up horrifying visions of human monsters who would commit any cruelty for the sheer fun of it. For the time being at least, it was the end of the tradition of the ever-open door in friendly villages where everyone trusted his neighbour. Women locked and bolted their doors and if somebody knocked, they peeped through the curtains before answering.

In factories and offices, their menfolk berated the authorities for allowing such a thing to happen.

'You don't build a tunnel like that overnight. They must have been at it for weeks! Where were the guards? That's what I'd like to know.'

'I'll tell you where the guards were. Down in Bridgend knocking back the pints. They're down there every night, fighting drunk some of 'em. It's disgusting.'

'Is it true what they say, that they have parties at the camp and ask the local women around?'

'So they tell me. No wonder the Germans do what they like. They haven't got time to go in the bloody compound to see what they're up to!'

Tempers were easily roused, and the German prisoner of war was not the most popular of men. There were strong grounds for believing not only that he received much better treatment than the British POW in Germany but, in some ways, better treatment than British civilians. In reply to questions in the Commons, Sir James Grigg, Secretary of State for War, had to admit that the rations of German prisoners in working parties exceeded the civilian ration – which not surprisingly infuriated the long-suffering British public. The Government's case was that they were abiding strictly by the letter of the Geneva Convention, which ruled that prisoners of war should receive rations equivalent to those of depot troops of the holding power, but the feeling in the country was that this was not so much scrupulous as ridiculous.

Down at Oldpark Farm fringing Margam Moors, Dillwyn Thomas was in no mood for nonsense. When a phone call came from the neighbouring farm of Eglwys Nennydd saying they thought they had some escaped prisoners in the store rick on the moors, he didn't hesitate for a moment. 'Bert!' he shouted in the yard. 'Get the pony and dray, quick!' Bert Jones, who worked with him on the farm, didn't waste any time either, and the two men paused only to grab a pike and billhook as tidy weapons in case of trouble. As they drove down the lane towards the rick they could see the boys of Eglwys Nennydd coming from the other direction – Willy Evans, Ned Hicks and Harry Prince. Suddenly they saw their quarry – two Germans who threw concealment to the winds and leapt over a hedge. 'Hey! Come here, you devils!' shouted Willy, brandishing a twelve-bore shotgun, but the devils showed no intention of stopping until he fired a shot over their heads to show he meant business. One of them stopped running then, and as they came up to him they could see he was a man of about forty who looked done in. They hauled him on to the dray and set off in pursuit of the other man, who was much younger and didn't like being captured at all. When they caught up with him he snarled Germanic oaths in a way that Dillwyn didn't find at all pleasing. 'Shut them up in the stable,' he said when they reached Eglwys Nennydd, but the daughter of the house, his cousin Nancy, felt sorry for the two men after their two nights' sleeping rough. She brought them cups of tea, but to Dillwyn's disgust the younger German poured his on the ground to show his contempt for this soft-hearted gesture. He was so incensed, in fact, that before the police arrived he saw to it personally that this stroppy young Nazi was 'roughed up a bit' to teach him a lesson.

It was about this time that John Marke was having the shock of his life. A lad of sixteen, he was waiting for a bus outside his home near Cefn Cribbwr when a military vehicle screeched to a halt and a soldier with a rifle leapt off the back and challenged him. 'I'm British!' said John plaintively, and was hardly reassured by the look of disappointment on the soldier's face. To his great relief, the attention switched from him to a point a hundred yards down the road where two men were emerging from a footpath with their hands on their heads. They were closely followed by soldiers guarding them at gunpoint, and the man who had challenged John brightened considerably as the Germans were bundled aboard and hustled away. It was all over so quickly that the lad could scarcely believe it had happened, but his grip on reality was reinforced by some objects he found at the end of the footpath – the Germans' maps and compasses, which he justifiably regarded as his personal spoils of war.

What he remembers best about the incident, however, is the click-click of the rifle bolt when the menacing-looking soldier challenged him. 'It frightened me,' he says wryly, 'far more than any escaping prisoners!'

He wasn't half so scared, however, as the housewife who was passing Bryntirion school, just outside Bridgend, when she heard the sound of twigs snapping and looked up to see three hefty Germans in army uniform. They ducked out of sight and after standing paralysed with fear for a moment, she ran for help. In the meantime, however, the prisoners made their getaway. 'I thought it best, being a woman, not to tackle them on my own,' she told reporters – who by this time were thick on the ground in Bridgend. Over the week-end the Fleet Street papers had sent teams of reporters and photographers into the sticks to cover a manhunt that was stealing some of the headlines from the Allied build-up on the Rhine. 'Planes Hunting 42 Escaped Nazis', said the *Daily Express* across three columns on its front page. The escapers were 'tough, devil-may-care youngsters and fanatical Nazis'. The *Daily Herald* preferred 'SS Men in Mass Jail Tunnel Getaway', while the *Daily Mail* hit on possibly the most emotive headline of the lot: 'Planes Hunt SS Men in Welsh Valleys'.

The *News Chronicle* feared the men on the run were out to do their damnedest. Under the headline, 'Escaped Nazis Plan Sabotage', they reported: 'A "last fling" sabotage campaign is believed to be the reason for the massed break-out . . . They know that the war is lost and that they have no chance of escaping from the country. It is considered very likely, therefore, that they decided to strike one last blow by sabotage.'

Before the week was out there were to be some tart remarks in London about the state of security at Bridgend, but it was the Cardiff-based evening newspaper, the *South Wales Echo*, that was one of the severest critics of the authorities in its 'Man About Town' column:

> We hope the War Office will hold a searching inquiry into the escape of the German prisoners of war from the camp at Bridgend. Not only has a large sum of money been spent on the recapture of the fugitives but hundreds of men of the Army, the Air Force and the police have been taken from their duties, from which at this juncture of the war they can ill be spared.
>
> There is another thing which cannot be overlooked. The escape of these German prisoners has undoubtedly created something of a state of terror amongst women and children in remote country districts over a wide area of South Wales. It is all very well for the authorities to broadcast their belief that the prisoners were unarmed, but hungry men are desperate men and we know that many of these Nazis would not shrink from committing any brutality.

It is incomprehensible to most people how the escape from the camp was accomplished without detection. A forty-five foot [sic] long tunnel is not 'scratched out' in a day. Either there were too few guards at the camp or those responsible for the safe custody of the prisoners have been too lax in the discharge of their important duties.

There are many indications that these men, hardened Nazis of the most virulent type, have been given an undue amount of liberty. They have, as might have been expected, taken this as a sign of weakness, and have been behaving in a disorderly manner for some time. If the truth of this statement is established by a War Office inquiry, there should be a tightening up of the control at the camp.

Britishers do not believe in being brutal to their prisoners of war of any nationality, but it is high time we recognized that with the majority of Germans the only argument they understand is force, and they should be clearly given to understand that it will be used unless they behave themselves while in custody.

We should see to it that they do not return to Germany believing we are 'softies' because we neglect to enforce necessary discipline.

EIGHT

In spite of the excitement of the chase and the fears of the vulnerable, life went on. Nothing was going to stop Peggy Thomas going to the pictures, nor Beryl Carpenter visiting her friends on a farm over a mile from her home.

Peggy lived on Stormy Farm, at the foot of Stormy Down, and like all healthy teenagers she enjoyed a night out. There was a Western showing at the Gaiety in Kenfig Hill, and she went along with her friend Mary Reynolds to see the action. The six-shooters on the screen, however, couldn't compete with the drama that followed. They hadn't gone far on their journey when three men emerged from a back lane, wearing heavy army greatcoats and with caps pulled low over their faces.

The girls nearly fell off their bikes in their surprise, for they knew at once they must be some of the Germans from Island Farm. As they pedalled on pretending nothing particular was happening, they had a whispered conflab.

'What shall we do, go to the police station?'

'Better not, they might see us. Let's go home, quick!'

And home they went like startled rabbits. 'Mammy, Mammy,' cried Peggy, rushing into the house. 'I've just seen three Jerries – do you think I ought to report it?'

S.S. Men In Mass Jail Tunnel Getaway

70 OUT—28 BACK

TOKYO'S HEART IS NOW ASHES

From CHARLES LAMBERT
"Herald" Reporter,
Washington, Sunday.

THE heart of Tokyo has been burned to ashes and smouldering ruin. A million people are homeless.

About 15 square miles of factories, offices and houses—with the small-scale domestic industry that was carried on in the larger Japanese homes—have been utterly destroyed by the myriad showers of incendiaries dropped by 300 Super-Fortresses in Friday's raid.

Aerial photographs taken by reconnaissance planes during the week-end show that not a single building remains intact in this vast target area.

Eight identifiable industrial targets lie in rubble heaps with a hundred other industrial plants.

The target area lay on each side of the Sumida River, but it was extended westwards almost to Naka River.

Shortening War

The Emperor's palace, which lay outside the area, was not hit.

The photographs show that Tokyo's fire barrier system, described in recent articles, simply did not work.

Searing volumes of flame swept across the large open spaces designed as barriers to spreading fires in the rebuilding of the city after the earthquake.

General Curtis Lemay, Commander of American Air Force based on the Marianas, from where the 300 Super Forts flew, said: "If the war is shortened by a single day, the attack will have served its purpose."

Officers and men under his command, he added, will pursue that purpose stubbornly.

★ Continued on Back Page

"*Herald*" Reporter, VALE OF GLAMORGAN, Sunday Night

SEVENTY Nazi S.S. men, soldiers, sailors and airmen broke out of a Bridgend camp this morning.

They made the getaway at 4 a.m. through a tunnel under three barbed-wire barriers as guards patrolled above them.

Throughout to-day planes and hundreds of armed soldiers scoured South Wales and the West Country. Late to-night 42 of the prisoners were still at large. Some of

them may be armed.

Sixteen were rounded up before they got far, but 54 escaped into the darkness and split into small groups. One is reported to have been shot but the extent of his injuries was not revealed to-night.

Soldiers, Home Guards, police and Civil Defence men were hurriedly organised into a great search army.

By this evening they had rounded up another 12.

The escaped men are nearly all officers, and include paratroopers, Luftwaffe and S.S. men.

"They are all tough—most of them young," said a police officer.

"They are likely to be low until nightfall and then we expect them to start prowling."

The drama suddenly switched to the Forest of Dean, where four of the prisoners, probably armed, were reported to have hidden after abandoning a car in which they made a getaway.

Forest Cordon

Reconnaissance planes were called in. They flew over the 100 square miles of the lonely Gloucestershire countryside in an effort to track the Germans.

Police, Home Guards and forestry men set a cordon round the Forest.

Attempts to steal transport under cover of darkness are considered highly probable.

Soldiers with rifles guarded every crossroads. Army parties combed the fields and dispatch riders with tommy-guns patrolled all side roads.

Freed By Russians—Returning

NEARLY 10,000 British, American and French ex-prisoners liberated by the Red Army are awaiting repatriation at Odessa, and 3,413 have already sailed for home.

Among those homeward bound is the British party of 170 officers and 1,221 other ranks.

Women and children who have been in Germany are also in this contingent.

Reuter reported from Istanbul last night that 1,600 freed Allied prisoners passed through that city yesterday.

There are still at the Odessa transit camp about 2,000 British, including 200 officers, 2,000 Americans and over 5,000 French, many of them civilians.

How Fleet Street broke the big news. The number of escapers was initially given as 70, a mistake soon corrected.

Plenty of humour in this vivid portrayal by a Hut 9 prisoner of a porridge-carrying guard.

(David Williams)

Two of the wall paintings by prisoners stored away by Bridgend
County Borough Council.

(David Williams)

The map of Wales drawn on a handkerchief which escaper Karl Ludwig was carrying.

Huts like this at Island Farm survived for 50 years before being demolished.

(BBC Wales)

Clearly marked in the escape hut – the spot where the tunnel started.

(David Williams)

Police and military confer at Candleston Castle, Merthyr Mawr. A rare photograph held by Joan Knights daughter of Supt. May (second from right).

A road block near Bridgend.
(Western Mail and Echo Ltd.)

Four of the escapers return to Bridgend in 1976 – Hermann Schallenberg, Hans Hartzheim, Werner Zielasko and Helmhart Perl.

(BBC Wales)

The man who master-minded the manhunt – Police Supt. William C. May.

(Joan Knights)

…et Sale Exceeds **4,000,000** Copies Per I…

…S MILES FROM MAN…

**LING
…ES:
…UTE'**

…AY NAZIS

…eral Patton's
… the German
…fighting west
…reported.

…s has already
…way between
…e Americans
…érman traffic
…ap.

…r of General
…d highway in
…s troops are

…d nine-tenths
…n miles south
…uth.

…ute, and that
…hours.   They
…including 15

…first time," the
…" the Americans
…in considerable
…a force a decisive
…w about to emerge
…gebirge Mountains
…lain."

PST, RUDOLF, WE'VE TUNNELLED OUR WAY OVER—WHAT'S FOR LUNCH?

'Merciless Bombing': New Warning

GEN. EISENHOWER DOOMS TWO CITIES

1,000 Nazis Die For Desertion

GERMAN Radio announced yesterday that 1,000 men and officers of the Wehrmacht have been executed by the mobile courts-martial, the

M ARMIES

"MERCILESS bom-
bardments will be

In the early hours of yesterday
morning Bomber Command made

**An…
At…
Thr…**

W…

…liberated
…answer to
…in authori…

…Mem…
…of these
…of whea…

…Members
…mental Co
…Shipments,
…Roosevelt,
…meeting to-
…be in favo…
…allocations a
…reduction of
…relieve Eur…
…emergency s
…tained in B…

…British B
…fially deni…
…Washington
…Britain wa…
…necessarily
…spite of the
…tated area…
…They decla…
…fortunate po…
…some food
…needs, but w
…and will co…
…the relief of
…Instead of
…this, we sho…
…work out th…
…atically.
…"It is a ba…
…be met, and
…Britain and …

…CONTR…
…One Ame…

This *News of the World* cartoon makes play of the suspicion that top Nazi Rudolf Hess was living in luxurious captivity in Britain.

Since they were only twenty yards from the police station when they first saw the men, three more swastikas would have gone up on Superintendent May's map a lot sooner than they did if the girls had reported it right away but when you're only seventeen, it's an understandable lapse to run straight home to mother. Perhaps, though, it was poetic justice when Peggy was woken up that night by a thunderous knocking on the door. A torch flashed in her father's face when he answered it, and a voice said: 'We're searching your outbuildings for Germans. Have you seen anything suspicious?' It was some RAF lads, performing their duties zealously – for it was a welcome break in routine to be wandering the countryside looking for Nazis. Next day the Free French arrived from the same air base, marching along in single file singing a popular song of the day: 'Come Out, Come Out Wherever You Are'. The sheer comedy of the scene appealed hugely to Peggy, for as she says, 'I doubt if they'd have seen any Germans even if there were any there, because all they were doing was staring at the boots of the man in front as they strode along line astern!'

The Germans at Kenfig Hill had covered only four miles in two days, which made them far less successful than the ones who frightened Beryl and her friends at the top of Tumble Hill, on the outskirts of Cardiff. Keeping their heads down by day and following an eastward path by night with the aid of their compasses, they were no less than twenty miles from Island Farm when they stumbled across the six girls making their way home arm-in-arm. It was an eerie experience which Beryl recalls in meticulous detail – first the scuffling of leaves behind them and the guttural voices in the dark, then the shock of being literally trodden on by one of the Nazis, whose boot caught the back of her heel. It was a shock for him too, because the girls had kept so quiet that he didn't realize they were there. 'Achtung!' he said softly to his comrades, and, as the girls stood there petrified, the Germans crossed the road swiftly and disappeared into the trees on the other side.

There were voices in the dark at Pencoed, too, where the woods which had given Gwyn Leyshon and his pals such an unexpected adventure the day before provided a good hiding place for other escapers. They came from a field at the back of the hostel housing 200 men working at the Bridgend munitions factory, and PC Harry Hopkins and Special Constable Selwyn Ellwood went to investigate. As silently as tracker scouts, they crept along the line of the hedge listening to those quiet, guttural voices, trying to establish how many Germans were in there and wondering if, like those already recaptured, they would come quietly. In the event, they did – a catch of four which they marked up gratefully at search HQ.

The whereabouts of the impudent prisoners who had dumped Dr Milne's car in the Forest of Dean, however, were still a mystery despite a vigorous search involving British and American troops and hundreds of volunteers. One possibility that occurred to the authorities was that the Germans might try to elude them by swimming across the Severn Estuary at low tide, so patrols kept a careful watch in the vicinity of Blakeney. 'The escaped men are believed to be looking in a dishevelled condition, and it is probable that earth and clay still adheres to their clothing as a result of their passing through the tunnel,' reported the *South Wales Echo*, which went on to warn its readers that many of the Germans roaming the countryside were English-speaking, 'while others who can't speak English may know certain stock phrases which would allay suspicion in a chance encounter with civilians'. This was probably true enough, but since a nation at war is encouraged to see things in terms of black and white, it undoubtedly strengthened the impression that the German prisoners were a lot of diabolically cunning Krauts who had ruthlessly taken advantage of their captors. The *Echo*'s cartoonist, J. C. Walker, was incensed enough to take the escape as his subject for three consecutive days, and his cartoons expressed the popular feeling that the British were a nation of softies in their treatment of German POWs. One of them showed a smiling Rudolph Hess, who had been a captive since flying to Britain from Germany in 1941 on an eccentric peace mission, smoking a cigar and drinking Scotch as he read a newspaper bearing the headline, 'More German Prisoners Escape From British Camps'. The cartoon was headed, 'What Fools Some Mortals Be'.

The famous British bulldog spirit was thoroughly roused by the injustice of it all, and it was exemplified by the morale-boosting activities of the Assistant Chief Constable of Glamorgan, Luke J. Beirne, and his wife. Mr Beirne, an eighteen-stone Irishman, believed in keeping up the spirits of the searchers, a policy heartily endorsed by Mrs Beirne, who took it upon herself to ensure that the men scouring the countryside for the unspeakable Bosche were supplied with adequate refreshments. While her husband called in at key points to check on progress, she was busily doing her bit in the mobile canteen, handing out cups of tea and sandwiches and cheerfully chatting up the chaps. It was quite like old times, the spirit of Dunkirk and the blitz and all that, only this time it was reinforced by the comfortable knowledge that barring an unthinkable catastrophe victory was just around the corner. By now many of the policemen who were out hunting Germans were dog-tired, having been on duty for forty-eight hours with scarcely a break.

There was to be little sleep for Bill May on that Monday night, however, for his head had hardly touched the pillow when the phone rang. It was one of his officers giving him the kind of news he was dreading: a woman had been shot in Porthcawl by a German soldier on the run.

The story, as it emerged, seemed depressingly straightforward. Just before midnight Frank Jones, a motor engineer working late in his garage with his friend George Lewis, had heard a shot fired at the back of New Road. 'I wonder if it's the German prisoners?' exclaimed Mr Lewis, and the two men rushed out but at first could not see anything. They decided that it must have been a car back-firing, and returned to the garage. It was then they heard voices and, going back for a second look, they found a woman lying on the ground with a tall man crouching above her. She was Mrs Lily Grossley and the man was her husband Howard, a Canadian soldier. The couple were fairly well known in this part of Porthcawl, where they had been lodging for the past fortnight with their two-year-old son. An anguished Grossley said his wife had been shot by one of two German soldiers who had attacked him and then run away across some nearby allotments. The woman had a bullet wound in the chest and an ambulance came to take her to Bridgend hospital, where she was receiving blood transfusions.

'Bad isn't it, sir?' said a police officer sympathetically.

'It's worse than bad,' replied Superintendent May grimly. 'It's one of the worst things that could possibly have happened.' For apart from the iniquity of the crime itself, there was the question of what violence it might spark off in the men searching for the escaped prisoners. So far they had been admirably restrained, although some of them believed passionately that the only good German was a dead German. If they now thought there were armed Nazis going about the towns and villages shooting at defenceless civilians, anything could happen.

To Bill May, however, there was something about Grossley's story that didn't quite ring true – and after thirty years' service in the force, he had an instinct for such things. 'I don't want anything connecting this shooting with German prisoners in the press,' he told his men. 'Do you understand? Not a word.'

The word of rumour, however, was outside his control, and by midday it had spread the news of the crime as far as Bridgend, where the cohorts of the press descended on him.

Unlike many other senior policemen at the time, Bill May did not regard journalists as his natural enemies. In fact he prided himself on his good relations with them, and held daily press conferences during the search to keep them fully in the picture. But he knew he was up against it now. Those Fleet Street reporters had been sent down to get the news, and the shooting of a woman by a German POW was very big news indeed. How could he persuade them not to run the story? He decided to make a direct appeal to them.

'It's true that this woman has been shot,' he said, 'but the circumstances aren't at all clear at the moment. I'm not convinced that any German prisoners of war were involved in this incident. The point is that if you boys publish the story as it stands in the papers tomorrow, there will very likely be a state of panic in the civilian population. People will be thinking there are twenty or thirty armed Germans running around shooting people down without a moment's hesitation. I know you've been sent down here to get your stories, but I appeal to you – please lay off this one just for today, so that I can make further enquiries. I'll give you a full statement this time tomorrow, I promise you that.'

The Fleet Street lads shifted uneasily in their chairs. Concealment went against the grain, especially when it came to a story this size.

'That's all very well,' said one of them, 'but what if the story is true? Don't you think people ought to be warned about two dangerous Germans going around with guns?'

'I agree,' said May. 'If that's the case it would be our duty to do so. But I think our main duty now, as responsible citizens, is to prevent public panic. I think this story may well be a fabrication.'

'It sounds like a cover-up to me,' said a disgruntled reporter. 'I suppose you know, Mr May, that the authorities down here aren't too popular in London as it is? It's appalling that all those men should have been allowed to escape in the first place. Questions are being raised in the House. Why should we suppress this story just to save you further embarrassment?'

'Gentlemen,' said May quietly, 'I think you know me better than that. I've given you the fullest possible co-operation since you've been here, and I'll continue to do so. But I repeat – if this accusation is made public now, there'll be panic in the streets. You know as well as I do that we've got men with guns searching for prisoners of war they believe to be unarmed. It's still my belief they're unarmed, in spite of this report to the contrary. But if they read in the press tomorrow that a German has deliberately fired a shot at a defenceless woman, I wouldn't like to answer for the consequences – and I don't think you would either.'

The reporters conferred, and reached a decision. 'OK, Mr May,' said their spokesman. 'We agree to lay off the story just for today. But if it leaks out, God help us.'

They trooped out, leaving a thoughtful Bill May behind them.

'What's the latest from the hospital?' he asked.

'She's still critical, sir. It looks like touch and go.'

'And what's she saying now about Grossley's story?'

'The last I heard, sir, she was confirming that she'd been shot by a German.'

But as the day progressed, some new facts emerged. It turned out that the patient wasn't Mrs Grossley at all, but Lily Griffiths, an unmarried woman. She and Grossley had been living together for four years – which proved nothing in itself except that the story, as it first came to light, was wrong in an important detail. The character of Grossley was becoming clearer, too. He had a vile temper and was prone to violent outbursts when drunk, which was pretty often. He had a way with him, however, and if he did knock back the double Scotches in the Porthcawl pubs, so what? A soldier on leave is entitled to a fling. He was a big, strong man whom people did not care to cross, and when he heard about the mass escape from Island Farm he had reacted belligerently. 'Get me my pistol from my room,' he told the sixteen-year-old son of the house where he and his 'wife' were lodging. The lad did as he was told, and watched excitedly – if somewhat nervously – as the Canadian showed him how it worked. 'If I come up

104

against any Krauts I'm gonna need this,' said Grossley, putting the gun in his pocket.

Bill May inwardly digested these facts, then made a decision. So far he had left the investigation to his detectives. Now he went to the police station at Porthcawl to have a word with Grossley himself.

Over in the Vale of Neath, they had other things to think about. The hard-pressed local police, who were pretty thin on the ground, were on the look-out for a hardy bunch of Germans who were believed to be heading in that direction after crossing the mountain from Cymmer. 'We'd been searching the mountains without any success,' said Andrew Jones, who was the police inspector at Glynneath. 'It was hard work because we only had six regular constables covering a very wide area – the younger ones were all in the armed forces. We called out all the specials and war reserves to join in the hunt, and there was no stopping them! Some of them even wanted to take out the rifles we kept in the police station, but I said no – we'll stick to our staffs, boys. But believe me, the specials would have known how to use those rifles. They were old soldiers from the First World War . . .'

It wasn't an old sweat who first spotted the Germans, however, but a workman who saw them sloping around the sidings of Aberpergwm colliery. He was so quick raising the alarm that three of them were arrested among the trucks. The other two were more elusive, for they hid among the bushes in the grounds of

Aberpergwm House, which was occupied at this time only by a caretaker. He ardently joined in the hunt, beating the bushes with a cudgel and peering into the leafy darkness of the rhododendron. It wasn't long before the two men were captured, and all five were taken to Glynneath police station.

The smell of cooking greeted them. Inspector Jones's wife, May, was busy in the kitchen.

'They're tired out and hungry,' he told her. 'Can you make them a cup of tea, do you think?'

'Hungry, are they? Well, they'd better have this cake I've just baked.'

They looked in amazement at the Dundee fruit cake she put in front of them in the chargeroom. This wasn't the kind of treatment they were expecting. One of them, however, refused to let even a crumb pass his lips. He scowled and harangued the others for accepting British hospitality. When he started physically pushing them around, it was too much for Inspector Jones. He had him locked up in the cell on his own until the military arrived.

Once he was out of the way, the remaining four relaxed. One of them spoke English well, and told the inspector that he was very familiar with this part of Wales as before the war he had taken part in cycle races between Swansea and Brecon. He knew the old parish roads better than some of the locals and it was clear that, with or without a map, he would have found his way around the hills of north Glamorgan. Inspector Jones was surprised by the prisoners' thirst, for they drank glass after glass of water, so he asked him for an explanation. Wasn't there plenty of water in the mountain streams to quench their thirst?

'We daren't drink that!' was the reply. 'We were told in the camp that all the water in the open in Britain had been poisoned . . .'

The inspector remembers this man well. 'He was very fair, about five foot ten in height. A friendly sort of chap. He told me they came out of the camp in groups of five: one who could speak English, one who could fly an aeroplane, one who could navigate so that they could get away if they reached the coast, one skilled in first-aid and an SS man. The SS man with this lot stuck out like a sore thumb. He was the one I had to put away in the cell. The others were fair-haired, Anglo-Saxon types from West Germany, but he was from East Germany, very dark. He was nasty, too. Every time the cyclist fellow spoke to me he blackguarded him in German. The atmosphere changed completely once he was out of the way. They were all a bit scared of him.

'I didn't interrogate them because we were told not to do that. Our orders were simply to keep them there till the military arrived. They just sat around and were no trouble at all. When the interrogator arrived I told him about putting the SS man in the cell and he went in there on his own. I don't know what happened exactly because I kept out of the way, but I can remember the officer coming out looking pleased with himself and saying, "I think I could do with his Iron Cross . . ." '

NINE

The art of crime detection, like the art of war, requires the element of surprise at crucial moments. So as Superintendent May sat opposite Howard Grossley at Porthcawl police station, going over his statement point by point, a part of his brain was testing the merits of a plan that had occurred to him as a way of getting at the truth of the Lily Griffiths shooting. Certainly, it was clear that something more was needed than a prolonged questioning of Grossley, for the man had his story off pat. He had been going home with Lily along the path behind New Road when two Germans 'rushed' at him. One of them shot Lily. They had then run away across the allotments.

'I see,' said May eventually, with the air of a man who has satisfied himself that the essence of the truth lay revealed. 'Well, there's just one point I'd like to clear up, if you don't mind.'

'Of course,' agreed Grossley. 'I'd be glad to help.'

'Come outside here a minute, then.' And May went into the corridor, followed by a bemused-looking Grossley.

'It's about the way those two Germans rushed at you. I want you to show me exactly how they did it.'

Grossley didn't move.

'Come on. Pretend I'm you and you're the Germans. Show me how they came at you in that lane.'

Suddenly all Grossley's self-confidence vanished. He just stood there, looking helplessly at May.

'Thank you, Grossley,' said May quietly. 'I think that will be all for now.'

He was convinced now that Grossley had shot the woman himself, but something more was needed to convince a jury. A detective stayed at Lily's bedside, and back in Porthcawl the bullet that had passed through her body was found embedded in the wall of the house opposite. It fitted Grossley's gun.

The next day Bill May had a call from London. It was from a major in the Canadian Army Provost Corps, who had just read a paragraph in the *Star* headed 'Woman Shot During Walk'. It read: 'Mrs H. Grasseley [sic] is in Mid-Glamorgan Hospital suffering from a serious bullet wound received when walking along a lane near her home in Porthcawl. Police do not associate the incident with any of the escaped German prisoners.'

True to their word, the Fleet Street morning papers had not published a line. But this down-page snippet in the evening paper set the major moving fast.

'I've just been reading a newspaper report about a shooting in your part of the world,' he told Superintendent May. 'A Mrs Grassley is the unfortunate victim, I gather.'

'Not Grassley. That's a mistake. It's Grossley. At least, we thought her name was Grossley but it appears now she was merely living with a man of that name.'

'Would that be Bombardier Howard John Grossley of the Canadian Army, by any chance?'

'That's him. Do you know him then?'

'Know him? You bet we do. He's a deserter and he'll shoot his way out of anything.'

Grossley was charged with attempted murder next day and before the week was out a dying Lily Griffiths made a new statement before Superintendent May, a magistrate and the magistrates' clerk, who sat by her bedside as she painfully whispered the words that condemned her lover. The essence of her testimony was that Grossley, fed up with his shifty way of life and the way he sponged off her, said she would be better off without him and threatened to 'finish' himself off. He pulled out his gun and she tried to stop him using it on himself. In the struggle it accidentally fired.

Four days after the shooting, Lily Griffiths died. In spite of her death-bed statement, the jury at Glamorgan Assizes decided that Grossley (who had a wife in Canada) had deliberately killed her during a quarrel. He was found guilty of murder, and went to the gallows.

The unravelling of this mystery imposed a further strain on men who, since the escape, had driven themselves very close to exhaustion. After three full days of chasing Germans, however, they had the satisfaction of knowing that forty-six men were back behind the barbed wire of Island Farm, leaving twenty-one enjoying – if that is the right word – their freedom.

'It is extremely unlikely,' remarked the *Western Mail*

confidently, 'that any of those believed to be still in Glamorgan will be able to break out of the strong cordon thrown around the entire area.'

Although the paper was not to know of the Germans' fears of poisoned mountain streams, it accurately pin-pointed their need for water as perhaps their biggest problem.

'Thirst may well lead to the prisoners' recapture,' the paper conjectured. 'While they possibly have sufficient food to last for two or three more days, it is thought that they will search for water, so special watch is being kept on possible supplies.'

A close watch was also being maintained on Cardiff, Swansea and other ports in the Bristol Channel 'in case an attempt is made by the men to reach Eire'. This was a sensible move, because the Irish Republic was the destination of the escape group that included Carl-Heinz Brockmeyer. Small in stature and something of a wag, his chirpy manner disguised deep anxieties about his wife and two sons back home in Germany. He did not know if they were dead or alive, for he had been enduring all the horrors of the Russian campaign in 1943 when news came through of thousands of civilians dying in the three-day bombing of his home city, Hamburg. 'I wanted to reach Ireland so that I could go home as soon as the war ended,' says Brockmeyer, who later became a civil servant. 'We were making for Port Talbot and had a naval officer with us so that we could take a boat and sail to Ireland.'

After going through the tunnel they headed west

through the darkness. When dawn came they found themselves on the edge of a quarry, where they were driven into hiding by the sound of aircraft. They assumed the hunt was up, and that these were reconnaissance planes on the look-out for such fugitives as themselves. Shortly afterwards, another sound frightened them even more – that of shooting in the fields around them. As they lay low, the gunfire came closer and they heard men shouting and a dog barking. When five figures appeared on the sky-line, they were in two minds about what to do. Should they run for it, or outface these countrymen – for to their relief, it was obvious that they were neither soldiers nor policemen – in the hope that they might go away? In the event nobody moved. 'They looked at us and we looked at them, and no one did anything,' recalls Brockmeyer, relishing the comic element in the situation. It was the dog that made the most decisive move. With an apt commentary on the inscrutable ways of mankind, it calmly lifted its leg.

Brockmeyer and his friends stayed in the quarry until nightfall, when they stretched themselves, took up their haversacks again and pressed on. The skies were clear and, having schooled themselves to navigate by starlight, the constellations told them they were heading in the right direction. They left the fields and tramped along the road into a town they took to be Port Talbot. They mingled with a crowd spilling out of a cinema, but their luck was not to hold much longer. Someone spotted approaching soldiers and they split up precipitately, Brockmeyer diving over a garden wall and crouching there until he cautiously raised his head and saw the coast was clear. By now he had only a solitary companion, and the two men made their way through the streets of a town where, at the fag-end of a Welsh Sunday, there were few people to be seen.

Suddenly Brockmeyer spotted an old gaslight, ornate and thoroughly Victorian. It aroused the poet in him.

'Look at that lantern,' he murmured in German. 'Isn't it romantic?'

'Hey, you there!' bellowed a very unromantic voice from the gloom of a doorway. 'Put your hands up!'

Four sturdy members of the Home Guard emerged, wondering darkly what these sinister Nazis had been muttering under their breaths.

Like Brockmeyer and his pals, the two Germans captured near the village of St Nicholas had also been making for dockland – only in their case it was the much bigger and busier dockland at Cardiff, where the notorious bars and brothels of Tiger Bay lured many a good serviceman away from devotion to duty. They were taken to the small, grey-stoned police station, where the local bobby was a burly rugby player, Charles Hutchings, who after his retirement lived in the Cardiff suburb of Whitchurch. 'A mobile policeman picked them up at about eleven o'clock at night,' he said. 'I questioned them a bit, but they refused to give me their names or anything. All they said was that they were German officers and on their way to Cardiff docks. They could both speak good English. I was under the impression from what they said that there was a ship in Cardiff waiting to pick them up.' Was he sure about that? 'Well, that was the impression I had.' He was impressed by the number of cigarettes they were carrying – 'dozens of packets of Woodbines stuffed into the pockets of their jackets'. They also had four tins of corned beef apiece – 'but,' he added with a smile, 'they didn't take them all back to Bridgend with them'.

This was understandable, because even a humble plate of corned beef was a luxury. The meat ration was a meagre ls 2d a week (6p), and there was talk of cutting it to only 10d or 11d because of a world meat shortage combined with the demands of what were known as the 'liberated countries' of Europe newly wrested from Nazi rule. A White House announcement that Britain would receive only 25 million pounds of meat from the USA between April and June, compared with 207 million pounds between January and March came in for criticism in the press, and there was sardonic reportage of a refining in the diet of German POWs in American camps, designed to conserve foods which looked like becoming scarce even in the land of plenty. The new daily intake of 3,560 calories included the use of sausage in place of fresh meats, which in future would be limited to hearts, liver and kidneys, and whenever possible fresh vegetables would replace the tinned variety. There were few tears for incarcerated Germans, however, and the *South Wales Echo* returned to the ever-popular theme of soft treatment in a leading article:

How does the world shortage of food and the starving thousands of victims of German avarice fit in with the requirements of the Geneva Convention concerning the treatment and the diet scales of prisoners of war?

There is no question of starving our enemies as they have treated prisoners and forced slave workers, but some of the dainty foods are likely to disappear from the menu, especially fresh meats, tinned fruits, vegetables and butter.

Worried housewives here at home are asking why, since the enemy has broken the Geneva Convention – and worse – he should be fed on foods which they can't get by standing in queues.

The emotive nature of the subject can be seen in the fact that a twenty-six-year-old butcher's assistant in Brighton was driven to suicide by the constant nagging of customers. And in Leicester a man supervising a gang of POWs on land drainage was understandably annoyed when he found they had corned beef to eat, whereas he only had bread and jam. He bartered cocoa and coffee and cigarettes for tins of 'bully beef', but was taken to court and fined £58 for this illicit piece of private enterprise. With this kind of thing going on, it's no wonder the *Echo* concluded that 'German POWs should be put on a diet no better and no worse than the civilian population has enjoyed for more than five years.'

One of its readers, Mrs W. Gallagher of Abertridwr, put it more strongly: 'I say, give them even less than the civilians of Britain get. If they had the trash that our prisoners of war get we would not have half of them on our hands now. My brother has been a prisoner of war for five years. "The Red Cross saved our boys from starvation" are the words of two prisoners of war who have come back to this valley.' (A reference to the Red Cross food parcels distributed in POW camps.)

Public feeling being what it was, it was just as well that the men who rounded up the prisoners in South Wales did not suspect that some of the food they were carrying had been stolen from British stock at the camp. What puzzled Walter Jenkins most of all, however, was the amount of cigarettes they had tucked away in their boxes and kitbags. As a war reserve constable he escorted four of them back to camp from Aberdare police station, and he recalls: 'They all had those round tins of fifty Gold Flake. They offered me some too – I could have been rolling in them if I'd wanted them.'

The men had been captured on Rhigos mountain and it was obvious to anyone who knew this bleak, windswept terrain that they were irretrievably lost. They were travelling away from the coast towards the Brecon Beacons and once they strayed from that road they could soon have found themselves up to their knees in the mud of a treacherous bog. Perhaps they found the mountain air exhilarating, for they were in good spirits when Walter Jenkins arrived at Aberdare in his Bedford police van to take them to Bridgend.

'Have you found their maps yet?' he asked the inspector.

116

'Maps? What maps? They haven't got any.'

'I'll be surprised if they haven't, sir. I've taken quite a few of these boys back to Bridgend and they've all had maps of some sort.'

'Well, this lot haven't got any, I can tell you that. We've searched them.'

'But have they been searched thoroughly, sir?' persisted Walter.

'Look here,' said the exasperated inspector, who did not much enjoy being told his job by a mere special. 'If you think they've got maps go down to the cell and look for yourself.'

'Very well, sir,' said Walter respectfully. And down he went.

He returned a few minutes later and spread the prisoners' khaki scarves on the table. A map was drawn on one side of them, and the constellations by night on the other. The inspector didn't say a word.

The Germans had blacked their faces in the hope of being mistaken for Welsh miners, and one of them used blacker language when Walter put the handcuffs on him. 'Me captain!' he protested, but this didn't impress Walter in the least. The officer struggled, which possibly accounts for the fact that his skin was nipped when the cuffs were clamped on. 'He screamed like a pig and shouted "Me report you War Office!" ' recalls Walter phlegmatically.

The officer was still fuming when he put them aboard the van and sat opposite them in the back, uncomfortably aware that he was shut off from any contact with the driver. 'I was armed with a revolver and they were handcuffed to each other but you still felt anything could happen,' says Walter, who was glad to see the back of them when he turned them over to the guards at Island Farm. He was impressed by their supplies of food, which included sugar and margarine and even bread rolls, and impressed too by those beautifully drawn maps. 'They were well-prepared for the escape, there's no doubt about that,' he says reflectively. 'It was the Welsh mountains that beat them.'

The idea of posing as workmen wasn't exclusive to this particular group of escapers, for three of the Germans even had the effrontery to board a workmen's bus just before midnight at Cwmgwrach in the Vale of Neath. What gave them away wasn't anything untoward in their appearance but the fact that they sat in complete silence. In the London Underground this would have been perfectly normal behaviour, but in the friendly Valleys it was the height of unsociability for three new workmen to keep themselves so thoroughly to themselves. The regulars on the route looked at each other, then had whispered consultations, and finally one of them walked up the gangway and murmured something to the driver.

The three Germans weren't to know when the bus veered off its usual route. But they got the message when it stopped outside a police station.

This, in its way, was one of the lighter moments of the chase, and there were many others. Ted Spencer, one-time village bobby at Laleston, remembers a prisoner being recaptured with an accordion strapped across his shoulders. 'I think he was preparing for a march or something,' he says drily.

Then there was the Porthcawl special constable who was standing on guard at a lonely spot on Stormy Down one night when he heard a movement in the gorse a dozen yards away. 'This is it,' he thought, and grabbed the starting handle of his car for protection.

Unnerved by the continuing silence, he flashed his torch on the 'German' – and found himself looking into the ruminative eyes of a cow.

A woman alone in the house with five children had a bad scare when she plucked up enough courage to go outside to the coalhouse, for as she bent over the bucket someone grabbed her shoulder.

'I've got five children,' she pleaded, too terrified to turn to face her assailant. 'If you want any food then take it, and my purse is on the sideboard – but please leave me alone!'

There was no response, and she soon discovered why. Her jumper had simply caught on a hook on the coalhouse wall.

In the seaside resort of Aberystwyth, 100 miles from Bridgend, fifteen-year-old Emlyn Edwards was on his way home from the weekly meeting of the Sea Cadets with his pal Henley Thomas when he saw two shadowy figures on the quayside.

'It's those German prisoners,' hissed Emlyn, a lad of lively imagination. 'Let's tell Dad, quick!'

They ran to his home in Rheidol Place, where his father, George Edwards, listened phlegmatically.

'If you thought they were Germans,' he grumbled, 'what's the use of you both coming here? One of you should have stayed to keep watch.'

He grabbed a poker and the torch assigned to him as an air raid warden. Grim-faced, they made their way back to the harbour.

'There they are,' whispered Emlyn, 'Just by that wall – look.'

With poker at the ready, his father flashed his torch on the enemy – and quickly switched it off again. The courting couple, caught in its glare in what can be tactfully called a compromising position, hastily adjusted their dress as the patriots beat a retreat.

Sister Elsie Woosnam, however, didn't find anything to smile about when some recaptured prisoners were brought to Bridgend hospital for treatment. She first noticed them when she went into the corridor outside the plaster room, where she was on duty, and saw two British soldiers with guns guarding the entrance to the X-ray department. A few moments later she was asked to hold the patients' limbs in position while they were X-rayed, as they didn't seem to understand English. 'I went in with my usual attitude to a patient, you know, smiling reassurance, but I felt it wasn't wanted. They were so cold and arrogant and disdainful. I felt almost like an intruder. Later some of them were brought into the plaster room and I remember putting a splint on a man, which meant I had to reach across his chest. It was unnerving because he was as still as a statue, and the others were the same. They didn't really look at you. They stared at some fixed point. It was as if you didn't exist.'

Even a nurse is human, and when she had to take the plaster off the foot of one of the prisoners her annoyance showed itself in an attitude so unlike her normal one that it's still vivid in her memory. 'I remember thinking to myself, "If I nip you it doesn't really matter." It's because I couldn't be my usual self with patients. Do you know what I mean?'

TEN

The enthusiasm of the fugitives for the chase varied considerably. Some were glad enough to be captured after a couple of days' sleeping rough, with rations running low and the chances of getting clean away looking increasingly remote. But the three Germans who went to earth on Mynydd Margam were of sterner mettle.

The mountain, rising behind Port Talbot to heights of 1,000 feet and extensively wooded in parts, was the kind of place where a hunted man could evade capture for weeks if he were resourceful and tough enough. It consisted of nine square miles of rough terrain, intersected with narrow, secret valleys refreshed by bubbling streams and clear pools. The spot they hit on as a hideaway was near Graig Goch Farm, on the lower slopes of the mountain, and amid the scrub and bracken they made a den which reminded them of happy summers in the Hitler Youth in the 1930s, when the Führer made them feel that the world was at their feet.

With the sunshine of that warm spring day on their backs, they looked across the Bristol Channel to the faint outline of the Devon coast. Beyond Wales, England. Beyond England, France. A so-called 'liberated' France. Germany seemed a long way off . . .

Still, they must not despair. And if they could not get back to Germany, there was always Ireland . . .

There was only one thing that spoiled their little idyll, and that was their increasing hunger. Their rations were fast running out, and living off the land was easier in theory than in practice. They cast longing eyes in the direction of Graig Goch Farm, picturing the sides of bacon hanging in the kitchen and the fresh eggs and milk on the breakfast table.

It was an irresistible sight, even though it existed only in their imaginations.

One evening Glenys Evans, who lived in the farmhouse with her sister Megan, was just about to go upstairs when she saw a German officer in the hall. 'He looked at me and I looked at him. Next thing I was out like a light. I fainted from sheer fright.'

It would have been bad enough seeing one of the dreaded Nazis by day, but what made it worse was that this was late evening and she saw him in the eerie light of the candle she was carrying. 'We didn't have electric light on the farm in those days.'

The farm workers, who had been having a bite to eat in the kitchen before going home, searched everywhere for the intruder, but he had vanished like a will o' the wisp. What if he came again? The sisters hit on the answer. He had probably been looking for food, so they would supply it themselves. That night they left bread and cheese and other titbits – even some home-made jam – on the window sill of the pantry, just as in more superstitious times people would leave food out for the fairies. They also scattered sand below, so that if the food did vanish overnight they would have some idea who had taken it. Next morning the food was gone, and there was the mark of a military-looking boot in the sand.

The soldiers came up the mountain looking for the Germans, but they had gone to ground as cunningly as a trio of old foxes. As darkness fell they went away, and the two sisters felt the loneliness of the night creeping up on them. Their brother worked the farm by day and went home to his wife at night, and it was to him they turned for help. They persuaded him to soak a rag in paraffin, then set it alight in the bracken before he left. The resulting blaze, they surmised, would bring the fire brigade clanging up to the farm, and they would be alone no longer.

He agreed, and the fire brigade duly arrived in all its glory. The only trouble was that the Germans had beaten the flames out themselves, and much to the sisters' chagrin the firemen turned around and went home.

The prospect of being smoked out like mice from the harvest stubble, however, did not endear itself to the Nazis, so under cover of darkness they moved west across the mountain, skirting an Iron Age fort before climbing through steep woodland, where they snatched a few hours' sleep. They pressed on at dawn until they reached the top of a high ridge, which was quite far enough for the eldest of the three men. Grey-faced and exhausted, he was complaining of pains in the chest, which met with sympathy from one of his companions but impatience from the other, who wondered why he had saddled himself with such a weakling. This man, tall and Saxon in appearance with fair hair and light blue eyes, looked longingly at the harbour at Port Talbot, now clearly visible. So near, and yet . . . How could he possibly succeed, with a sick man on his hands? Should he ditch the other two, and go it alone? The unexpected dilemma troubled his tired brain as he stretched out on the springy grass, with the skylarks pouring out their song overhead as if they lived in a world where the only loyalty was to life itself. He dozed for a while, and when he awoke the morning was well advanced. He looked at his sick comrade, then buried his head in his hands. Nothing was simple.

Nearly a mile to the south, between the Germans and the sea, Emily Rowland was busy with her chores that afternoon at Tyle Gigfran Farm when her fourteen-year-old son Jeffrey dashed into the house.

'Mam! Gran wants you! She's waving the red cloth!'

Emily knew at once what he meant. When her mother waved the red cloth out of the bedroom window, it meant she wanted them urgently up at Llan Tanygroes Farm.

'I wonder what's wrong? Quick, get your father!'

In a few minutes, Jim Rowland was on his way. He knew the significance of the red cloth, too. If it had been a white cloth he wouldn't have been in half such a hurry. This simple code – white for 'come up when you can' and red for 'come right away' – was an infallible means of communication between Llan Tanygroes and Tyle Gigfran at a time when neither farm could boast a telephone. It was necessary because both farms were isolated, and it was possible because Llan Tanygroes, high on that ridge, commanded a perfect view of Tyle Gigfran.

As Jim reached the bottom of the rough track leading up to Llan Tanygroes, he found his mother-in-law, Mrs Elizabeth Davies, hurrying down to meet him.

'What's up?' he called, as she drew nearer.

'Germans,' she said breathlessly. 'Three of them from Bridgend. Willy caught them in the fields and he's got them there now.'

'Good God. Is there anyone up there with him?'

'No. That's why I came to get you. I'm a bit frightened for Willy. They seem harmless enough, but . . .'

'Don't you worry now. Leave it to me.' And he began running up the track.

'Be careful now, won't you, bach?' she called anxiously.

'Of course. Always am, aren't I?'

Elizabeth sighed and hurried on to Tyle Gigfran. She was a countrywoman of the old school, baking her own bread and drawing water from a well sunk into the floor of the dairy in her farmhouse. She didn't easily panic, but escaping Germans were something new in her life.

When she told her daughter Emily what had happened, they both made tracks for Llan Tanygroes right away, with dark-haired Jeffrey hurrying ahead on horseback. His twelve-year-old sister Grace wasn't to

126

be left out either, so it was quite a family party that arrived to find the Germans washing and shaving in the stream that ran through the farmyard.

'Any trouble, Willy?' asked his wife anxiously.

'None at all. They're too tired to be any trouble.'

'Poor dabs. I wonder how long they've been up on the mountain?'

'A few days, by the look of 'em. I'll tell you one thing. They're starving. How about giving them something to eat?'

'Of course I will. You don't have to ask me that, do you?'

'Well,' said Willy, with a twinkle in his eye, 'they are Germans, after all.'

'I don't care what they are. They won't go from here without something in their stomachs.'

But she knew her duty in other directions, too. She sent a farm boy who had turned up in the meantime pelting helter-skelter down to the village to fetch the police.

Willy was explaining yet again how he came to capture the Nazis.

'They were standing over by the fence. I crept up to them with the pitchfork but when they turned and saw me they didn't make a fight of it at all. I think they'd had enough. One of them had, at any rate. He looks pretty ill to me.'

When they'd finished shaving, the Germans trooped wearily into the old-fashioned farmhouse. The sick man said a few words to Jeffrey in halting English and, to the boy's embarrassment, he cried a little. 'I have a son in Germany,' he said, 'the same age as you.'

Mrs Davies spread a clean white cloth on the table and brought in boiled eggs, home-made bread thickly buttered and pots of jam. The Germans wolfed it down, then lit their cigarettes. The tallest of them, resigned now to his fate after so much heart-searching, wandered out of the house, followed closely by Jim.

'Don't worry,' he said in a quiet, disdainful voice. 'I'm not running away.'

He leaned against a gate, looking down the narrow cleft of the Brombil Valley to the sea. Jim asked him how he came to speak such good English.

'I went to college to learn English so that I can be a regional governor when Germany wins the war,' he said coolly. 'Who knows? I might come back here.'

'If you go to some parts of Wales,' said Jim jocularly, 'you'll have to learn Welsh as well.'

'No, my friend. We won't let them speak Welsh. Only German and English.'

While Jim was digesting this, the German went on: 'The trouble with Britain is that there are too many parasites. At the end of the war they will all be collected up and taken to the labour camps in Germany. They will learn how to work there.'

He paused. 'Tell me, where does Aneurin Bevan live? It's not far from here, is it?'

'Well,' said Jim, surprised by the question, 'his constituency is in Ebbw Vale but that's a fair way from here. Why do you want to know?'

The German shrugged. 'He's a good friend of our country. He will help us get to Ireland.' *

Not long after this astonishing statement, the police arrived. As they huffed and puffed up the hill, wiping their brows in the heat of the afternoon, the blond officer sneered, 'What a fit lot of men!' They were led by an inspector who brandished a gun. The German was not impressed.

'One . . . two . . . three . . . ' he counted carefully. 'Eleven of you and a gun to capture three unarmed men. Not bad, huh?'

'That's enough of that,' snapped the inspector, 'Put your hands up.'

They marched him back into the house, where the policemen searched the Germans for weapons. Emily realized with a sudden chill that it had never entered their heads that these men might be armed.

Before they left, the Germans thanked their hosts for their hospitality and said they would like to pay for the food. 'We have the money,' they explained, and offered a pound note.

'Here, I'll take care of that,' said the inspector, snatching it from them. 'Where did you get this, anyway?'

'We didn't steal it, I assure you,' said the insolent one. 'As a matter of fact I sold my watch to a guard at Bridgend.'

* A piece of wishful thinking inspired, perhaps, by Bevan's frequent clashes with Churchill in the Commons. As a lifelong socialist, Bevan was certainly no friend of Nazi Germany.

'Did you now? Well, you'll get your watch back and the guard will get his pound.'

The Germans were handcuffed to one another and hustled away. The party was over.

It was over, too, for the prisoner recaptured by a CID sergeant in Cardiff – although, by the look of him, it hadn't been much of a party at the best of times.

'His clothes looked as if they'd been rescued from a dustbin,' said Gordon Prosser, who had reached the rank of inspector by the time he retired from the force. 'In fact I thought he was a tramp at first.'

Sergeant Prosser was out looking for thieves in Cyncoed, a posh area of the city, and when he saw this dishevelled character he told the driver to pull up.

'I asked him who he was and he just stared at me blankly. I repeated the question but still got no reply. Suddenly the penny dropped and I said to him in German, "You are a prisoner of war from Bridgend, aren't you?" He replied, "Jawohl." '

The sergeant had learned German while serving in the army in Silesia and Germany early in the 1920s, and although he hadn't used it for years he still found it serviceable enough to keep up his end of the conversation on the way to the police station.

'To tell you the truth I felt a bit sorry for him,' he confessed. 'He was no more than five foot seven and about forty years of age. He had no money, no food, no map – he wasn't prepared at all for an escape. He cadged some pipe tobacco off me and seemed quite pleased when he found it was Virginian. I asked him when he'd eaten last and he said he hadn't eaten at all that day. Poor chap. He wasn't a very good example of Hitler's *Herrenvolk* . . .'

They put him in a cell at Cardiff's central police station to await a military escort, and he beamed his gratitude when Sergeant Prosser produced a steaming cup of tea and a plate of sandwiches from the canteen. It was all very friendly – so friendly that the soldiers, when they arrived, seemed almost like boorish intruders.

As they took him away, the German gave the sergeant a friendly wave. 'Vielen Dank, mein Herr! Aufwiedersehen.'

It was all sweetness and light in Richard Howard Davies's signal box too. He was alone there at dead of night at Cwmavon, just outside Port Talbot, when he heard someone climbing the wooden steps outside.

'It didn't worry me,' he said. 'It could have been one of my regular callers. The local policeman would often drop in for a few words, unofficial, like. Or it could have been a shift-worker calling in for a chat.'

Instead it was a German prisoner of war who raised his arms as soon as he was inside and said: 'Kamerad.'

'He just walked in and stood there looking pitiful,' said Richard. 'I thought, there's someone even worse off than I am! I gave him a little bit of grub – Spam sandwiches and a bit of cake. He'd have eaten the tin as well, I think! He looked really washed out. He couldn't speak any English so we talked to each other in sign language. I said "Heil Hitler" and put my hand up in the Nazi salute, just to get some idea what he thought of it all, but he shook his head and said "Nein". We had a smoke together and he stood in front of the fire and dried his clothes. When the policeman arrived he took his helmet off to show it was nothing official, like, and the three of us sat there as if we'd been pals for years. "Well," said the bobby at last, "I've got to take him away now." "You're not going to put the handcuffs on him, are you?" I said. "Certainly not," he said. "He's been in handcuffs long enough," and away they went with no trouble at all.'

ELEVEN

If some of the escapers had known what kind of a reception awaited them back at Island Farm, they might have made more effort to keep their freedom. 'I've got to be careful here,' said an ex-serviceman who was a guard there at the time. 'There were no atrocities, such as kicking anybody in the groin and so on. But they were helped along, shall we say, with the butt of a rifle. And if their elbows dropped when they had their hands on their heads, they'd be knocked back up with a rifle butt.'

The prisoners' own recollections are more vividly expressed. They say they were made to run the gauntlet from the camp gates to the guardroom, with soldiers standing to left and right beating them with their fists and rifle butts. There was some psychological warfare, too, for the first sight that met their eyes in the guardroom was a heap of blood-stained clothing. It belonged to Lieutenant Tönnsmann, the prisoner who had been shot in the shoulder. The guards knew the newly captured Germans would not yet have found out how the escape had been discovered and the exact circumstances of the shooting, and so were able to scare the living daylights out of them.

'We've shot one of you bastards for escaping,' they

said, 'and if you want proof of it those are his clothes. We're going to do the same to the whole fucking lot of you. We'll have you up against the wall, one by one.'

It was pure bluff, but it worked. The recaptured men thought their last days had come.

'They lined us up against the wall with our hands above our heads for a long time,' said Karl Ludwig, the SS man recaptured by the village policeman at Llanharan. 'The soldier guarding us was waving his rifle and shouting and swearing. Suddenly the gun went off and the bullet went into the wall just an inch or two above my head. The sergeant shouted "Bloody fool!" and took the rifle off the soldier and put another man in his place. I think he was an inexperienced soldier, that first one. He didn't seem to know what he was doing.'

Ludwig says he left the guardroom after the interrogation minus two front teeth, which were knocked out by a rifle butt. Helmhart Perl remembers the return to Bridgend, too. 'The first thing we had to do in the guardroom was undress completely. We then had to sit down on the floor with the legs stretched out absolutely straight, with the back perhaps about three centimetres from the wall. Just try doing that for about ten minutes! It's terribly painful. When the muscle pains were so bad that we leaned back against the wall almost automatically, we had a beating – which as a naval officer I didn't find particularly pleasing. We were kept sitting in this position for about an hour. I don't want to make too much of this because it could well be that the officers knew nothing about it, and we certainly don't want to reproach them for it. It was simply an action by the lower ranks, but all the same it was a fact. Of course, I quite understand the annoyance of the guards over the mass break-out, which undoubtedly caused trouble for the camp personnel, and during captivity I met some wonderful people among the British officers. They did their utmost from humanitarian motives on behalf of the prisoners, and I still respect them today. But following this escape, the camp personnel at Island Farm did not behave as one would have expected of the famous British fairness.'

One theory put forward by the escapers is that the guards' anger stemmed partly from their fear that they would be sent to fight the Japanese as a punishment for not preventing the break-out. Brockmeyer remembers a guard saying in pidgin English, so that there should be no misunderstanding, 'You escape and we Burma!' They could be forgiven for wishing to avoid a share in the jungle war with the Japs, but the possibility of the British Army dispatching such poor physical specimens to the Far East at that late stage seems, in retrospect, pretty remote.

A British officer who was one of the senior camp personnel at the time, now living pleasantly in retirement in north London with his army life far behind him, was asked about those beatings. 'I remember I had to warn one chap after the escape,' he replied. 'I saw him get the butt of his rifle into the backside of a prisoner as they were going across the compound. I told him, "If you do that again you'll be on a charge." But you can understand the feelings of the chaps. They'd been confined to barracks because of the escape. The Germans couldn't expect . . .' He left the sentence unfinished.

And the events in the guardroom? 'Yes,' he acknowledged, 'they were stripped and made to stand in the guardroom. I think there may have been a bit of rough-housing and as far as I remember they complained to the Swiss about their treatment, but when the delegation from the Swiss Red Cross came down they had no complaint.'

Brockmeyer's account of the events after his recapture by the men who overheard his remark about the romantic gaslight has a rather sad humour about it. 'Two jeeps came along, and two motor-cyclists wearing helmets, in other words military police, and we were taken to Port Talbot police station. They showed us a list and I saw several names had already been crossed off and I thought to myself, "Thank God, we aren't the first ones to be caught!" We had to go through almost the same procedure as my colleague Perl has explained, and afterwards we were taken to the camp theatre. On the way there we had to run the gauntlet. I got a kick in the backside and suddenly I was standing in the middle of the concert hall, and there around me were the comrades who had been captured before me. We were all very depressed. Our hopes had been so high, and here we were back behind barbed wire. Then I turned around and saw the piano. I thought to myself, "Man, you'll have to play something now, you must really get things going again!" So I sat down and played a piece I had known by heart since the age of ten . . .'

It was 'The Parade of the Little Goblins', and it revived the spirits of his comrades so much that he played it again. In the next three days Brockmeyer went through his whole repertoire several times over, but his performances came to an abrupt stop when the British officers, deciding that their recalcitrant prisoners should not be allowed the luxury of music, ordered the removal of the piano.

On the Thursday following the escape, Mr Arthur Henderson, Financial Secretary to the War Office, faced the music himself in the Commons. After his brief statement, in which he said that a court of inquiry was being convened, Mr E. J. Williams, the Labour Member for Ogmore (a constituency which included Bridgend), asked if the court would be considering the actual siting of the camp.

'No sir,' said Mr Henderson, who had equally economical replies for the two MPs who wanted to know what kind of implements were used in the escape, and how the men were able to dispose of such large amounts of earth without anybody spotting them. 'We had better wait until we have seen the report of the court of inquiry,' he said.

Mr James Griffiths (Labour, Llanelli), who later became the first Secretary of State for Wales, asked whether the Minister himself would consider this was a suitable site, in view of the fact that the inquiry might not cover the point.

'We will look into every aspect of the question,' Mr Henderson promised.

Mr Edgar Granville (Liberal, Eye) took the chance to urge the Minister to hasten the arrangements for receiving a deputation of MPs 'who have continually called attention to Nazi activities among prisoners of war'.

No doubt many members had read the 'Opinion' column in the *Daily Express* that morning, which dealt with the Bridgend escape in typically trenchant style.

These two sets of figures make close comparison:

Seventy German prisoners escaped from Glamorgan camp in March 1945.

76 Allied prisoners escaped from Stalag Luft III in March 1944.

54 of the German escapees have now been recaptured.

50 of the Allied prisoners were shot by the Gestapo.

And with these sets of figures the comparison ends and the contrast begins.

The story of the hunt for the escaped Germans shows that they have had good food. Some were found with bully beef and condensed milk saved from their rations (when, by the way, did British civilians last own spare bully beef?)

Contrast the conditions of these Nazis with the treatment of the British prisoners just released by the Red Army. They were treated, they say, 'harshly but correctly'. They eked out German rations with Red Cross food.

Britain and America, who have captured over a million Nazis since D-Day alone, have adhered strictly to the military law that prisoners shall have a food ration 'the equivalent in quantity and quality to that of the depot troops of the detaining power'.

They should make the standard of comfort of German war prisoners correspond with the known standards of Allied prisoners in Germany.

In an adjoining column, William Hickey worked out the odds against a prolonged getaway by German prisoners in Britain as 9,000-1. But the Communist *Daily Worker* (fore-runner of the *Morning Star*) was in no mood to look for silver linings. The previous day they had run a report which amounted to the severest criticism of the authorities to appear in the press. Under the four-column headline 'Escape-Camp Nazis Goose-stepped Through Village', their unnamed reporter wrote that he had arrived in Bridgend to find the place 'seething with indignation at the way in which seventy German prisoners, most of them the worst type of Nazi officer thugs, have been allowed to escape'. His report continued:

Ever since the ordinary German soldiers were turned out some months ago and the camp converted to an officers' POW camp, local inhabitants have known that there has been trouble.

The chairman of the Bridgend Trades Council, Mr Ivor Davies, told me that it has been evident that the prisoners were guarded with a laxity which has amazed the people, many of whom have relatives in German prison camps.

As an instance of what has been going on, Mr Davies told me what happened when one of the Nazi officers died in the camp a short while ago. The whole camp paraded in the market place for the funeral, and then goose-stepped through the town, giving the Heil Hitler salute.

'Their arrogant behaviour and their contempt of the prison guards,' he said, 'made us all believe that their treatment was far too lax. But we were told that the reason for the special privileges accorded to them was that they were entitled to special treatment under international convention.'

The Welsh Committee of the Communist Party has protested at this laxity.

'The Welsh people,' Mr Idris Cox, secretary of the committee, told me, 'are alarmed by the thought of Nazis roaming at large in their midst. We demand stricter control in such camps and the suppression of Nazi influence in them.'

The people here are also indignant at the slowness with which they allege the military authorities at Western Command have tackled the job.

A local Home Guard officer told me that if they had had the necessary petrol, it would have been possible to throw a cordon of at least 2,000 ex-Home Guards around the area within six hours.

Application was made to the Western Command for the necessary petrol with the support of the local police, but the application was refused and as a result valuable time has been lost.

The involvement of the Home Guard on an official basis, however, may not have been quite so easy as the *Daily Worker* made out, because Dad's Army had been formally stood down the previous autumn, when George VI took the salute at a final parade in Hyde Park. The 'odd position' of the Home Guard was remarked on by the *Star*, whose man in Bridgend reported:

> After the breakout the police asked hundreds of local Home Guards to help in the hunt. Then they were told by the military they must not do so except as civilians.
>
> I was told on good authority today that the Cabinet alone could authorize the recall to duty of the Home Guard now that they are 'no longer required to perform active duties'.
>
> There can be no quick local action anywhere – even if a German suicide squad arrived in Britain. All Home Guards, no matter how well-trained in the use of weapons, are in exactly the same position as untrained civilians.
>
> It was pointed out that if the Home Guard – who still have their uniforms – acted as a body under officers or NCOs, they would be breaking all the rules. No authority now is responsible for the issue of food, subsistence allowance or petrol for quick movement.
>
> It took more than red tape to strangle the enthusiasm of the Home Guard, however, and one battalion alone had 150 men in the field, manning observation posts and searching on foot, in cars and even on horseback!

TWELVE

By now only thirteen of the sixty-seven men remained
free, and they included the enterprising four who were
posing as Norwegian engineers. Shrewdly they had
judged that the British passion for hiking meant that a
quartet of healthy-looking individuals strolling about
the countryside in civilian clothing, with haversacks
slung over their shoulders, would not in itself be a cause
for suspicion, and they wandered around for two days
before deciding they had had enough. They were tired
and hungry, and they had to summon up all their
willpower to stop themselves despairing of ever finding
an aircraft to take them back to Germany. When they
saw a train in a railway siding, with the hissing engine
announcing an early departure, they needed only a
hurried consultation to decide to steal aboard in the
hope that it might take them somewhere near an airport.
Their exultation at escaping detection, however, was
quickly spent when the wagons started rolling, because
it was an ammunition train and they were sitting
uncomfortably on bombs intended for their homeland.
The irony of it did not escape them, but they were soon
more concerned with the discomfort. Though they
shifted and squirmed continually, there was no way of
avoiding the fact that this was a purgatorial journey.

Even when the train stopped at a station, they could not get out to stretch themselves for fear of detection.

They stuck it for two days and two nights, and then could stand it no longer. Next time it stopped, they decided, they would make a break for it. As luck had it, they were near a wood when the clanging wagons shuddered to a stop, and as quickly as their stiffness allowed they hurried into its depths with every muscle aching. Ah! the luxury of stretching their legs! They felt they'd been in that jolting wagon for weeks. When darkness came they had a good night's sleep, and the first sound they heard next day almost convinced them they were still dreaming.

It was the sound of aircraft engines. By a stroke of good fortune, they had ended their journey near Birmingham Airport.

They went to the edge of the wood and looked across at the planes silhouetted in the distance in the early morning sunlight. It was a sight they knew they would never forget. They were so overcome that, for a moment, none could trust himself to speak. Then they began talking excitedly, going over the plans they had made so carefully in captivity and which now, at last, looked like reaching their climax.

'Hans, remember! It all depends on you now!'

'Please, don't say that. You make me feel nervous!'

But Harzheim, chosen for the vital role of front man because in the opinion of the others he was the most plausible of the four in terms of speech and appearance, was ready for the challenge. Carefully he shaved his five-day growth of beard in the chilly water of a brook and picked the mud and leaves from his coat. The others stood back and meticulously inspected him.

'How do I look?'

'Fine! Like a real English gentleman!'

'But I'm not English, remember? I'm a Norwegian engineer.'

'Well! Like a Norwegian gentleman, then!'

They gripped his hand warmly and wished him good luck. And with a last check that he had the forged papers in his pocket, Harzheim left the comparative safety of their hideaway for the perils of civilian life.

It was strange being on his own. Prison life did not fit one for isolation. He felt exposed and vulnerable, and as he walked along the streets of a suburb his disguise seemed as patently false as that of a child in a fancy dress parade. Norwegian engineer! Who would believe him? Yet with every step his confidence grew, for he found that the people he met scarcely gave him a glance. They had their own lives to live, and the respectable-looking stranger was no concern of theirs. He began to breathe more freely and looked around with vivid interest at his surroundings. So this was England, wartime England! He noticed the early-morning queues for cigarettes and the headlines in the papers. More heavy bombing of German cities . . . ah, the sooner they were home the better!

He joined the queue at a bus stop and nobody took the slightest notice of him. When the bus came along he boarded it with pounding heart and sat by the window, staring out. He asked for the nearest stop to the airport and the clippie unquestioningly gave him a ticket. He thought of his comrades back in the woods, how they were depending on him. The adventures they had been through together! If they did fail at the last hurdle, it would be an honourable defeat. Yet he must not think of failure. And what were its consequences, anyway? An airport in wartime was a place of strategic importance, and a German officer wandering around it in civilian clothing ran a fair risk of being shot as a spy. He braced himself for the ordeal and silently went over his story yet again.

Now it was time to leave the bus and he sauntered towards the gates of the airport hoping he did not look half as nervous as he felt. Would he even get inside? The papers they had cooked up at the camp now seemed so crude a forgery that he was sure they would fail the vital test. The official who glanced at them, however, handed them back without a murmur and even gave him a friendly smile. Norwegians, after all, were welcome allies.

Inside the airport, Hans Harzheim still expected any moment to feel an ominous tap on his shoulder. But as the world went about its business and left him to his own devices, he relaxed. The English, after all, were not given to talking to strangers. With a bit of luck, he might not have to say another word.

For two hours he wandered around unmolested, memorizing the appearance of the planes so that he could describe them to Steffi Ehlert, the Luftwaffe pilot. He was away so long, in fact, that they feared his true identity had been detected, and when he returned to the wood with his mission accomplished they fell on him rapturously.

'Hans, you devil! We thought you were never coming back. What have you been doing all this time?'

'Doing? I've been arranging your transport home, of course. It takes time, you know,' he said coolly.

'They didn't suspect you?'

'Of course not. Why should they? I had my papers, didn't I? So obviously authentic!'

They laughed, delighted with themselves.

'Come on then, Hans. Don't keep us in suspense. Did you find a suitable plane?'

'Well, I hope so . . . '

He described some of those he had seen.

'That's the one we want,' said Ehlert eventually. 'You know exactly where it is?'

'Of course. If it doesn't fly away before we get there, of course.'

'Well, we'll have to risk that. We can't go back till it's dark.'

'You can fly that plane all right?' asked one of the others.

'Oh, I can fly it, don't you worry. With a bit of luck, this time tomorrow we'll be home.'

They imagined the welcome they would receive, and at the same time they dreaded what they might find. For they had been without news of their families so long.

'Come on, boys. Let's put our heads down for a while. We've got to be fit for tonight, remember.'

146

'Good idea.' And they lay down in their hideout with the afternoon sun filtering through the trees.

They fell into a fitful doze, only to be awakened by the snapping of twigs. They sprang up, but too late. Five farm workers stood facing them with shotguns. It was enough to make even a strong man weep.

It was the nationwide hue and cry that was their downfall. The five men had seen them in the woods earlier in the day and suspected them of being some of the escaped prisoners who had been in the news all the week. When challenged, their first concern was to bury their civilian top clothes in the woods in order to be taken into custody wearing only the prison uniforms they had kept underneath the whole time. Their understanding of the Geneva Convention was that so long as they did this, they ran no risk of being suspected of espionage and shot as spies.

Back in Bridgend, they wrote to Dr Milne apologizing for the inconvenience they had caused him by 'borrowing' his car and offering to pay for the petrol, but he declined with thanks and made it clear he did not wish to see them punished. In spite of their bitter disappointment at failing at the last hurdle, they had the satisfaction of knowing that in travelling over 130 miles from Bridgend they had gone farther than any of the other escape groups, apart from the two men recaptured the same day at Eastleigh, just outside Southampton. Lieutenant Sund Rols and his companion had been making for the docks, where they hoped to stow away aboard a ship, when they were seen leaving a goods wagon by a railway shunter at 6am. They disappeared behind some trucks and the railwayman raised the alarm. A search revealed two packs of kit in the wagon, which had arrived in the early hours from South Wales, and it was clear that it had been occupied for several days. A cordon was thrown around the yard, and the police even went to the trouble of calling in the aid of Mrs Nina Elms, who lived in the village of King's Sombourne, fifteen miles from Southampton. Her bloodhounds had a reputation for sniffing out troublemakers, and they had recently taken part in the hunt for the killer of a woman murdered in a Southampton alleyway. On this occasion, however, they turned up panting for action too late to have any chance of distinguishing themselves, for the two Germans were found hiding in a cement truck just before they arrived. Dusty and dishevelled, they surrendered to a railwayman blessed with the name of Pentecost, and in the final reckoning they had the distinction of being the most successful escapers in terms of distance covered, having put 150 miles between themselves and Island Farm Camp.

THIRTEEN

William Griffiths, a miner living in the Afan Valley ten miles north-east of Port Talbot, had followed the reports of the chase as closely as anyone, but the prisoners of war of Island Farm were far from his thoughts as he sat up late at night six days after the escape. He was, as he put it later, 'sitting by the fire enjoying a bit of peace and quiet'. The rest of the family were in bed, for it was past midnight, but he had been home only just over an hour after working his shift at Nantewlaeth Colliery and it was pleasant simply to relax and read the paper.

His peace was disturbed, however, when he heard footsteps passing the door of his little terraced house alongside the only road into and out of the valley. 'I thought at first that something had happened at the colliery and the men were being sent home, because nobody else would be out at that time of night. I dashed to the door but then I realized the footsteps were going up the valley towards the colliery, instead of down towards Cymmer. Then it suddenly dawned on me. Was it those prisoners of war?'

His uncle was living with them, and he went upstairs to have a word with the old chap to see what he thought about it. 'Don't you follow them all by yourself, now,' was the warning, 'you go and get some help first!' But what if it isn't them? thought Will as he went downstairs again. He'd look a right fool if he brought out the police only to find the footsteps belonged to some colliers after all!

'Damn, I ought to find out if it *is* them, at any rate,' he said to himself. But before leaving the house he put a souvenir of the First World War in his pocket – a revolver which, although it lacked ammunition, served to boost his morale. In a tight corner he could always wave it at the Nazis and convince them it was loaded, he reflected as he shut the door behind them. But his first enemy was the weather, because it was a night of Stygian darkness and driving rain.

After a while he could hear the midnight prowlers talking, though he couldn't see a thing. They were still too far away for him to detect what language they were speaking, so he shouted, 'Where d'you fellows think you're going at this time of night?' The only answer, after a few seconds' pause that seemed endless, was the sound of men running. 'I thought they were coming for me,' said Will, 'and I turned and ran like hell. I never moved so fast in all my life. A greyhound wouldn't have caught me. I remember thinking, if they *were* chasing me I'd beat them back to their escape hole in Bridgend! But suddenly I realized they were running in the opposite direction. They were even more scared of me than I was of them!'

He pulled up, with the thumping heart and bursting lungs of an untrained athlete thrown into the Olympics, and when he got his breath back he went to find a phone to ring the police. 'The nearest was at the colliery, so that meant crossing the river. It's a wonder I didn't fall in, it was so dark. And I was soaked to the skin already. A terrible night, it was. Anyway, I got to the phone and rang the police. They were in bed and I tell you, they were very loath to come out. In fact, the first thing the sergeant in charge said was, "Are you sure it's them now? We don't want a wasted journey." '

Will wondered why he'd bothered, but when the sergeant grudgingly said they'd be on their way he decided to continue his patriotic bit by keeping track of the Germans as best he could. So out he stepped again into the lashing rain, turning up his collar and pulling the peak of his cap low over his forehead. He thought of the fire he'd left and his uncle's advice, which seemed sounder now than ever. But Will wasn't the man to throw in his hand when a job was half done, so he grimly plodded on to Glyncorrwg, the mining village at the head of the valley where the road petered out and the mountains took over. It was the best part of two miles away, and the road had never seemed so long or so lonely. He was still half a mile from the nearest houses when a police car drew up alongside him with two sergeants inside.

One of them wound down the window and poked his head out. 'Where d'you think these Germans are, then?' he asked accusingly, as if Will had deliberately put them up to it to disturb the well-earned slumber of a British bobby.

'They could be up the mountain by now,' said Will

irascibly, 'or if not maybe they're in the railway carriages.'

The sergeant sighed. 'I suppose you'd better come along with us, then.'

'Thank you very much,' said Will, with a dryness that was not matched by the weather.

The railway carriages were always left overnight at Glyncorrwg station to form a workman's train first thing in the morning. There were three of them, and the thought of some hulking Nazis lurking inside them – and with guns, for all he knew – was not one to convince Will that he had done the right thing in leaving the safety of his fireside in a moment of patriotic madness.

'Well,' said one of the sergeants when they reached the station, 'I suppose we'd better take a look.'

They lumbered out of the car, and the three men started their reluctant search of the empty carriages. Revolver in hand, Will hoped the Germans weren't ones to shoot first and ask questions afterwards. A miner faced enough dangers in his daily life without feeling the need for false heroics.

The carriages were empty. 'Maybe they're up Pleasant View,' suggested Will.

'You reckon so, do you?'

'Well, they're bound to be somewhere, unless they've disappeared into thin air.'

Will had the distinct feeling that the policemen thought the prisoners of war were figments of his imagination.

'Let's take a look then.' And the three men trudged up to Pleasant View, where the cottages built by Victorian coal-owners climbed the lower slopes of the mountain that rose between the Afan Valley and the Vale of Neath. Up the winding road they went and on to the track beyond, where the icy rain stung their faces and their feet squelched in the marshy ground.

They had just about given up hope of catching anything except pneumonia when their torches picked out four figures slumped against a fence.

'They had their legs stretched out in front of them, beat to the wide,' said Will. 'I shone my torch right on them but they didn't move. They were whacked. And they weren't just hungry, poor dabs. They were ravenous. They were eating bits of toast, hard as anything. You could hit it with a hammer.'

If he had been hoping for a hero's ride home, however, he was soon disillusioned. The sergeant in charge bundled the Germans into the police car and set off for Cymmer, leaving his two companions to make their own way back. 'The least he could have done,' said a disgusted Will afterwards, 'was send a car back to fetch us.'

He had a cool reception when he got home, too, for his wife, who knew nothing of his midnight adventure, opened a sleepy eye and scolded gently, 'Up all hours of the night wasting light and reading . . .'

The tracking down of these four sorry fugitives meant that Superintendent May had good cause for satisfaction when he turned up at Bridgend police station on

Saturday 17 March and looked back on the crowded events of that week. The thick clusters of flags on the map in the operations room showed that sixty-four of the sixty-seven escapers had been recaptured, thirty of them within seven miles of the camp. The road blocks and search parties set up by the old Glamorgan Constabulary, which was absorbed into the South Wales Police in the reorganization of police forces in the 1960s, succeeded so well that only eight men managed to get out of the county – the four recaptured near Birmingham, the two at Southampton and two who were caught between the Severn Tunnel and Magor, in Monmouthshire. Over twenty prisoners were turned in by members of the public as opposed to police and military, and it was an enthusiastic pursuit by a civilian which led to the arrest of the three remaining escapers on that Saturday evening. He was Mr John Hopkins, a thirty-two-year-old farmer of Glais, near Swansea, whose wife and mother were going home along a mountain path when they saw some suspicious strangers on their land. One of them shouted something they did not understand, and when they told John about it he promptly went to take a look for himself. As soon as they saw him they began to run in the direction of the village, but they hadn't reckoned on having a rugby wing-forward – and a Welsh trialist into the bargain – on their heels. He overtook them without any trouble and asked them who they were, but they weren't in a mood for bluffing. 'Please – the police station,' they said simply, but as the hamlet of Glais didn't boast anything so important John settled for the

154

sub-post office, where the postmistress, Mrs Donne, gave them cups of tea while the farmer phoned the police. One of the Germans felt relaxed enough to boast he had been the first man through the tunnel, and smiled broadly when told they were the last to be recaptured. It was he who pronounced what is, perhaps, the best epitaph on the escape from Bridgend. 'It was good sport,' he said simply.

The *South Wales Echo*, which earlier in the week had been so severe with the authorities for allowing so many men to break camp right under their noses, now gave praise where it was due. Their Bridgend correspondent, Jack Barratt, wrote:

> It is now possible to see how a vast network was spread and tightened around the hunted men. From the moment the alarm was raised the burden was particularly heavy on the Glamorgan police force, upon whom rested responsibility for the safety of the civilian population.
>
> Never for a moment was there a let-up in the search. Regular police, war reserves and special constables worked unceasingly. Returning weary from one quest and about to go off duty, they volunteered again and again to go out and form new cordons around fresh areas in which prisoners were suspected.
>
> Many of the specials, unpaid volunteers, sacrificed their own businesses for days to keep on the job. The military and the Royal Air Force were just as untiring in sweeping huge areas and the co-operation between the various services was remarkably efficient.

Railwaymen, especially those in lonely stations and isolated signal cabins, deserve praise for their vigilance, and the aid of civilian volunteers was continuous. In fact, a whole nation was on unceasing watch. The result was that everyone, military, RAF, police, railwaymen and civilians, all shared in the captures.

The prisoners were men of high ability, the cream of the German Army, well trained in the arts of war and concealment. They had planned their escape with imagination and skill; they had the aid of elaborate equipment and were well stocked with food. But they were beaten.

The speed and efficiency with which the Germans were rounded up was in some ways a personal triumph for Superintendent William May, the man who had first drawn up a contingency plan for dealing with a mass-escape and then master-minded the operation when it came to putting it into practice. The Army, recognizing this, sent three brass hats to thank him when the last men were safely behind barbed wire again, putting on record their appreciation of the way that police and public had co-ordinated with the military. Privately however, Bill May felt that the Army had a lot to answer for in not detecting the elaborate preparations for the escape. 'The guards just weren't alert enough,' he says. 'I think they relaxed after the discovery of the decoy tunnel a few weeks before. They congratulated themselves on foiling an escape bid.'

FOURTEEN

After the round-up came the inquest. A court of inquiry was held in camera, and its findings were summarized in a secret document drawn up at Western Command headquarters at Chester. Dated 13 April 1945, it was issued to camp commandants 'in the hope that the collation and dissemination of information in this manner will be a help to all concerned in adding to the security of PW camps in this Command'. A note on the cover rather plaintively observed that 'certain of the comments may be criticized as being wise after the event, but many valuable lessons can be learnt from experience'. It was emphasized that as a secret document this 'will *not* be taken into the compound nor left in any place where a PW is likely to gain access to it or learn of its existence', which, in view of the escapes that had occurred, was perhaps not so superfluous an instruction as it appears.

Although the document dealt with the discovery of no fewer than seven tunnels in camps in Western Command in March 1945, it was the events at Bridgend which, not surprisingly, had the lion's share of attention. Sub-titled 'Mass Escape From No. 198 PW Camp Bridgend', this section reads:

During the night 10/11 Mar '45, 67 PW escaped from No. 198 PW Camp. The Court of Inquiry brought to light the undernoted items of security interest:

(a) The camp was occupied before the works services had been completed. This afforded the PW ample opportunities for taking and concealing material. It follows that new sites should if possible be searched and cleared before occupation by PW.

(b) The unsatisfactory perimeter lighting was the most important single factor facilitating the undetected passage of the PW out of the tunnel.

(c) One suggestion made was that inventory boards should be placed in huts. Stores and inventories could then be checked frequently and this precaution would tend to prevent the mutilation and improper use of stores such as tables, benches, etc.

(d) Some of the material used in connection with the tunnel may have been obtained from tables and forms, many of which were found to have been cut up, shortened and sometimes halved.

(e) The cover to one tunnel was apparently a piece of asbestos and the cracks joining it to the concrete floor were probably concealed by clay covered with dust or cement.

(f) An interesting fact is that work on the tunnel appears usually to have been done during the daytime. One German PW witness stated that on the two occasions he worked in the tunnel, it was during the morning, after the morning count.

Another witness stated that work could not proceed at night because it made too much noise.

COMMENT

(i) Occasional and irregular snap daytime roll calls would have at least discouraged PW from illicit day work and forced them to work at night.

(ii) In addition to 'noises off' a count of heads after lights out may reveal night tunnelling activities.

(g) Many of the escapees economized on food during several weeks prior to the break-out, in order to escape with a substantial amount of food.

(h) One witness stated that earth from the tunnel had been packed into bundles or sacks and a good deal of it had gone into some slit trenches inside the compound. It is considered that much of it was disposed of down lavatories.

COMMENT

Disposal of soil from tunnels is one of the big problems encountered by potential escapees. Although some of the soil is occasionally disposed of down lavatories, most of it is scattered or deposited in the course of general gardening work. It follows therefore that very close observation should be kept on gardens round PW huts and unusual activity thereabouts.

(i) Blankets were used in the tunnel to stop prisoners' clothes from getting dirty.

COMMENT

An occasional inspection of blankets would NOT be amiss.

(j) An iron spike and short-handled shovel were used for the work of excavation and an improvised skid with rope was used for the conveyance of soil during excavation. The rope for the skid was made from electric-light wire and tubing from ARP stirrup pumps.

(k) Improvised fan and air pipe for air-conditioning the tunnel were used. The vane was made out of a barrack-room bucket, parts of barrack-room tables or forms, and empty tins from the cookhouse. The air-conditioning tube was constructed from empty food tins.

(1) It was suggested that war dogs would have been used to greater advantage if they had been on patrol outside the WD boundary and well away from the men patrols.

(m) Improvised compasses with magnetic safety razor blades were carried by several PW.

(n) Compound Search Officers furnished the Commander with a signed certificate in respect of each search which they made.

COMMENT

An excellent idea.

The reference to work on the tunnel being done in the daytime conflicts with the ex-prisoners' own recollections that it generally took place at night, and it is clear that the Germans managed to conceal some important information from the court of inquiry. In particular, their lips were sealed on the question of soil disposal. The court cottoned on to the fact that some had gone into 'slit trenches' in the compound (presumably connected with the digging of the pit for the long jump) but failed to detect that this concerned only the first tunnel discovered before completion and not the one through which the prisoners escaped. There is no mention of the false wall in the escape hut and the observation that 'much of it was disposed of down lavatories' was merely a guess unsubstantiated by the prisoners themselves. The court was right in thinking that many men economized on food for several weeks before the break-out, but the plundering of the British food store just before the escape presumably went unnoticed. So did the fact that the prisoners had reduced the height of their beds to obtain more timber as well as mutilating tables and benches.

The other tunnels mentioned in the document were at Crewe, Cheshire; Ambleside, Westmorland; Llanmartin, Monmouthshire; and Penkridge, Staffordshire. At Camp 191 in Crewe two tunnels were discovered on 13-14 March, the first when some anti-Nazi prisoners spilled the beans on the eve of their departure to another camp. A search of a hut occupied by Luftwaffe officers revealed a tunnel which the Army admitted was 'ingeniously disguised'. Instead of digging straight down inside the hut, the men made cunning use of the fact that the floor was two feet below the level of the ground outside. They cut away a section of the wall and began their tunnel below ground level just outside the hut. The detached section was put on runners and moved back at the start of a digging session, to be returned to its normal position when the men knocked off. The mortar was renewed each time to conceal the entrance so thoroughly that it was located only by running a razor blade along the brickwork until it probed the softness of the fresh mortar. Other sophisticated touches were the construction of two air shafts for the fifteen-yard tunnel, one camouflaged as a rustic table outside the hut and another resembling an old tin that had been thrown away.

The second tunnel at Crewe was discovered the next day. It had a more conventional entrance beneath a flagstone. Like the first, it was lit by electricity, but the ventilation was obtained by 'binding together a large number of cylindrical food tins from which the bottoms had been cut out'. The comment that 'such tins when empty should be removed from compounds' sounds obvious, but was nonetheless necessary because the experience at Crewe, Bridgend and elsewhere shows that at this stage simple precautions against escapes were not being taken. 'In neither of the cases reported would it have been possible to discover the tunnels by tapping,' the document continued. 'In each case it was located by meticulous attention to detail, and probing.'

The tunnel at Ambleside was also detected as a result of prisoners informing on their comrades. They dropped vague hints that a plan existed for the escape of forty or fifty men, and it was clearly well-organized as the prisoners had made biscuits from toasted bread and cocoa. These had been concealed in sealed tins and small bags, complete with zip fasteners, made from towels. Ovaltine, tea, coffee, tinned food and butter had also been hidden in the huts. The tunnel was supplied with electric light from an adjoining boiler house, which was used as a workshop for the making of tunnelling implements. The comment here was that since shortage of food was one of the biggest problems for escapers, it was essential that no food should be allowed in their sleeping quarters and that there should be frequent checks of the ration store. The discovery that one of the prisoners had been in the habit of playing a concertina during the digging, thus covering any noise and enabling him to give signals to the diggers by the use of particular tunes or phrases, led to the suggestion that 'certain members of camp staffs be trained in the art of seeing without being seen'. Such an observer at Crewe 'may have noticed a certain sameness about a number of PW day after day, thus arousing his suspicions'.

The decision to watch the progress of the tunnel for a week after its discovery before taking action did not, however, meet with official approval. 'It is doubtful,' says the document, with the deadpan, unintentional humour it displays so often, 'if this procedure is desirable.'

At Camp 184 in Llanmartin, a few miles east of Newport, the start of a tunnel was found by a dog patrol in a group of huts in the corner of a compound. 'The entrance was outside one of the huts and against the wall, the intention presumably being to go under the hut and come out at a stream on the far side of the wire.' The more orthodox prisoners at Penkridge began their tunnel under a bed and it was found during a routine

163

search, the commandant being commended for his practice of moving men from one hut to another without notice. 'The more widespread this practice becomes the better.' They also approved of the camp commandant who, 'in order to conceal the fact that a search was being conducted, had all huts cleared of kit and bedding in order that they might be sprayed with disinfectant. This worked very well, and PW were quite ignorant that any search was being conducted.' If tunnels were suspected, 'it is essential for all kit, bedding, forms, tables etc to be removed from the huts,' the document adding that this was laid down in a standing rule that 'at least once weekly PW huts will be cleared of all kit, tables, etc. so that the whole of the floors are exposed to view' – an instruction which the camp personnel at Bridgend had not been alone in ignoring.

The ideas of the camp commandant at Ambleside were passed on for all to read, mark and inwardly digest. He considered that effective measures against escape attempts involved 'frequent visits to the compound by the commandant to sense the atmosphere and to accustom the PW to seeing him there'. Moreover, the interpreter should make himself readily available to prisoners: 'a great deal of information can be obtained if the PW are allowed to talk, as against being questioned'. And there should be 'unceasing and *unobtrusive* patrolling and vigilance by the provost staff, particularly during the night'.

The commandant of the camp at Knutsford, Cheshire, had some pearls of wisdom to impart, too. He advised the encouragement of the reading of escape books, 'which are extremely entertaining, instructive and appeal to all ranks'. There was even a list of recommended reading. A daily conference was held at this camp, at which 'security and protection is always discussed even if only for a few minutes', and at Camp 176, Oldham, 'all previous escapees and known likely escapees are paraded before the wardens, who are instructed to study them carefully with a view to watching and reporting upon their movements during their tour of duty'.

Prisoners were up to all kinds of tricks. 'At one camp a pound note and two pennies were found during the search of a PW being admitted to detention, hidden in a shoulder strap.' And the commandant of a base camp in Germany found that one man 'had coated the inside of an empty bottle of Brylcreem with an opaque substance or white paint, and had hidden a map of the district inside the bottle'.

The report continued: 'After the transfer of a PW from one camp to another, his effects were carefully searched and a cigar box which he had in his possession was handled and its weight found to be more than that of an empty box. Further examination revealed a false bottom carefully covered by the paper lining usually found in cigar boxes. The smooth side of the false bottom faced upwards. Under the false bottom in snugly fitting grooves were found three files and a five-inch saw blade. These did not rattle when the box was handled.'

There was advice for those soldiers who had the job

of escorting prisoners on their journey by train from one camp to another. 'A would-be "train jumper" will normally jump out from the right-hand side of the train looking in the direction in which the train is travelling, thus causing the escort to fire from the left shoulder. Escorts should be warned of this . . . An old trick is to hide behind the door of the toilet in corridor trains leaving the door open, thus conveying the impression that the lavatory is unoccupied.'

A recent complaint by a prisoner was seen as a reflection of the change in the war situation. 'He was afraid that being a staunch Nazi, the anti-Nazis were going "to do him in",' which made a change from the usual pattern of threats of violence by zealous Nazis against their less enthusiastic comrades. 'The German nature being what it is,' was the comment, 'intimidation is not unlikely whichever side predominates.'

The six-page document concluded with a paragraph obviously designed as light relief. Sub-titled, with heavy humour, 'Tailpiece – Sassenachs Beware', it read: 'PW who recently escaped stated on subsequent interrogation that they were headed North in order to join the Scottish Resistance Movement!' In the days of the Tartan Army, that does not look so unlikely.

What the unfortunate Lieutenant-Colonel Darling made of all this we can only venture to guess. Two months after the mass escape from Bridgend he was put in command of Camp 191 at Crewe, and in April 1946 he was made an inspector of POW camps. He died in 1949, just a fortnight after his fifty-seventh birthday.

FIFTEEN

The authorities didn't wait for the results of the inquiry before deciding what to do about the prisoners at Island Farm. Their answer was to transfer them elsewhere: not just the escapers, but all 1,600 officers.

They left on 31 March, two weeks after the last fugitives had been brought back to the camp – and, incidentally, Easter Saturday. After marching through Bridgend in high spirits, singing even more rousingly than they had on their arrival four months before, they boarded heavily guarded special trains bound for 'an unknown destination'. The local people wondered anxiously if they were going to be replaced by an equally troublesome crowd, but they need not have worried. Island Farm was about to undergo a complete change of character, for instead of being filled with bellicose young officers it became the home of some of Hitler's leading generals, who soon showed that while they breathed fire on the field of battle, in captivity they were as gentle as any sucking dove. The metamorphosis embraced even the designation of the camp, for instead of being No. 198 it became No. 11 (Special) German PW Base Camp.

For anyone interested in the human cogs in Hitler's war machine, a visit to Island Farm in the summer of

1945 would have been a fascinating experience. Here they would have found men like Field-Marshal Walther von Brauchitsch, once the proud commander-in-chief of the German Army; Field-Marshal Erich von Manstein, one of the Führer's most successful field commanders; and Field-Marshal Gerd von Rundstedt, commander of the German forces in the west until his replacement by Kesselring two months before Germany's unconditional surrender. Walther Dornberger was there too, a boffin with the rank of lieutenant-general who had played an important part in the development of Hitler's secret weapons: those V1 and V2 rockets known familiarly, if not fondly, as doodle-bugs, which claimed many lives in south-east England in the latter stages of the war. The list of prisoners at Bridgend in this new chapter in the camp's story reads, in fact, like a roll-call of the Führer's top brass: General Karl Demelhuber, Admiral Hans Voss, General Hasso von Manteuffel, Field-Marshal Ewald von Kleist, General Heinrich Eberbach, Admiral Hans Hartmann . . .

One who recalled the period well was Ted Lees, later a divisional fire officer in West Glamorgan. At the time he was Captain Lees, interpreter at Island Farm and, as such, a bridge between the captive generals and the British camp staff. He spoke German effortlessly, being German by birth himself. He retained vivid memories of seeing Jews beaten up on the streets of Berlin during his childhood, and his hatred of the Nazis ran deep. It was because of them that he became an exile at the age of twelve, for his father, who opposed Hitler, had such fears for his future that he sent him away in the care of the Quakers to be adopted by a British family. The year was 1933, and when war broke out Ted Lees (who took his name from the family who gave him a home in Manchester) joined the British Army. After an eventful war in which he was dropped behind enemy lines to engage in espionage, he had mixed feelings about going to Island Farm as interpreter: but he looked back on it as one of the most interesting periods in his life.

'Von Seidel, a Luftwaffe general, was the German camp leader,' he said. 'He was pretty clear, politically, as far as we were concerned. He must have been because he became a NATO general officer. Admiral Voss was liaison officer. His function was similar on the other side to mine. About half past eight he would come out and we'd have a cup of tea and a smoke together.'

But the man who made the most impression on him was Rundstedt. In terms of age and army service, this old warrior was the senior figure in the German ranks, and they acknowledged him as such. 'A word from Rundstedt,' said Ted Lees, 'and they would run.' He had been a general when Hitler came to power, and his relationship with the dictator was turbulent throughout the crowded years of the Third Reich. He was relieved of his command on three occasions, but each time given another because the Führer could not do without his military expertise. He had helped to plan and execute the invasion of Poland, pursued the beaten British Expeditionary Force to Dunkirk in 1940, taken thirty-eight divisions into Russia, tried to stem the

Allied advance after the D-Day landings and, finally, led the counter-attack in the Ardennes in December 1944. Now, in captivity, he looked a frail and disillusioned old man. Crippled with arthritis, he hobbled around with a stick and made sneering references to 'that little corporal' – Adolf Hitler.

He is remembered with something close to idolatry by some of the men who were prisoners of war with him at Bridgend. 'He was a very upright man. Very aristocratic. A man of the highest integrity,' said one of them, a factory manager only a mile or two from the camp. 'He was very much aware of his position inasmuch as he was the senior officer. In many ways he acted as arbitrator in the camp when a dispute arose. The military code said the top man always had the last word, and the generals stuck to that. They never called in the British to arbitrate. They always settled it among themselves.' This man, who was a sergeant in the German Army and thus one of the NCOs at Island Farm who acted as batmen and waiters for the generals, clearly remembers the sense of outrage among the prisoners when Rundstedt was named as a war criminal and sent to Nuremberg – although, eventually, he only gave evidence and was not made to stand trial. 'Nuremberg was a farce. A vendetta,' he said. Did he not think, then, that the leading Nazis were guilty of war crimes? 'I don't say they were not guilty, but there was no body of law by which they could be brought to trial. I was a young man at the time, and I remember how they tried to make us all feel guilty. But no German

170

could accept the idea of collective guilt. This was the greatest mistake the Allies made at the time.' When Rundstedt left the camp in May 1946 for Nuremberg, 180 generals showed he had their moral support by lining up and saluting him (military style, not the now out-of-favour Nazi salute). 'He came back from Nuremberg a broken man. The Americans weren't very polite to him. They stripped him of his insignia and to a man like that, it was like stripping him naked,' recalled the ex-sergeant, who went on to describe his own feelings at the time.

'When the war ended I was in a camp near Birmingham. The English camp commandant lined us all up on the parade ground, 5,000 of us, and told us Germany was defeated. It wasn't so much being told this, though that was bad enough, but the way it was done. He used words like genocide, he told us we were guilty of horrible crimes. It was a very traumatic experience. One minute you are so proud, the next you are dejected. You could crawl into a hole. Today I could set it against things like Vietnam, but I was a young man then and when you're young you have very narrow horizons. The only wound I have is that it was done in such a brutal fashion, being a sensitive man. To deprive a man of his pride. To make him feel like an outcast, a leper. That he's not fit to be a member of a decent society . . . It was very clearly put to you. Perhaps, in Germany you wouldn't have felt it so much. But being imprisoned, not having a way out. Not being able to run away. You had to listen. Had to stand to attention.

Having to say yes sir, yes sir, and wanting to spit in his face . . . You were made to feel you belonged to a people who were not fit to inhabit the earth.'

He remembers how they were all forced to see films of Belsen. The idea was to confront them with this evidence of Nazi bestiality, to prove beyond all doubt what was being done in their name, but it did not have quite the desired effect. 'I didn't believe it,' he said simply. 'I don't think any of us did at first. We thought it was just Allied propaganda.' And today? He paused before replying slowly: 'I accept that it happened. But even now I think the numbers have been exaggerated.'

When he was allowed out of the camp on parole, he went with mixed feelings because he feared the reception he would be given. 'I was quite surprised when the civilians didn't express the same opinion as the military. It gave you back a certain amount of self-respect, that people would talk to you. That they would treat you like an equal. I came to know a family in Bridgend. I worked in their garden – he was a teacher. He was very trusting. He would go out into the town and I would be left in the house by myself. I found that very elevating, the fact that a man would trust me. That he was not afraid I would wreck the house or something while he was out. It was the little things which at the time meant a great deal.'

This was the period when there was great pressure for the 're-education' of German prisoners of war. 'There were no political lectures or anything like that. Re-education took place really because one saw how democracy worked. When you started communicating with people on the outside – farmers or people in the streets. Re-education is like converting a man's religious beliefs. It doesn't happen overnight.'

The authorities sent intelligence officers into the compounds to question each prisoner on his political beliefs, the idea being to weed out the more virulent Nazis and send them to special camps for re-training. One man engaged on this work at Bridgend was Otto John, a German lawyer who had been involved in the unsuccessful bomb plot against Hitler in July 1944. Now, with the war over, he was a willing tool of the British in their attempts to destroy Nazi influence in the prison camps. But he found it hard going, because with Hitler dead and the Third Reich in ruins, few Germans would admit to any Nazi beliefs. Ted Lees remembers him saying wearily one day, 'You know, it's marvellous. Out of 100 people only Demelhuber said he was still a Nazi.' This was General Karl Demelhuber, of the Waffen-SS, once commander of the 16 Korps. Rundstedt himself, however, had objected to the presence of Manstein and Brauchitsch at Bridgend, because they were 'tainted politically'. At his request, they were moved elsewhere. He wanted the camp run on purely military lines, without any Nazi overtones. 'Having a bit of peace and quiet – that's all he was concerned about,' said Lees. 'In fact he used to talk about his Hotel Island Farm . . . '

There were some high jinks in the 'hotel' now and then. When some generals went down with a mysterious disability which was classified as hypertension, it was found that their high blood pressure was due to the habit of holding 'cocktail' parties where the strong drink consisted of Camp coffee drunk neat, with a little sugar. 'Von Rundstedt put a stop to that,' said Lees.

There was no objection, however, to the more serious-minded activities at the camp, such as the classes which the prisoners arranged among themselves. With Dornberger giving lectures on rocket development and professors teaching higher mathematics, it was the nearest thing to a university education many of them were ever likely to experience. The urge for self-advancement extended even to some of the British guards, but their sights were sometimes set at a lower level: there were illiterates among them who were taught to read and write English by German prisoners of war.

Ted Lees recalled the tension in the camp at the time of the Nuremberg trials. 'I don't think they had an ounce of sympathy for the top Nazis, but they objected to regular army officers standing trial. Basically the feeling was that they had obeyed orders, as any professional soldier would have done. If they hadn't they stood to be shot. If some things were done which shouldn't have been done, it wasn't their fault. Remember, blind obedience made the German Army what it was. They were ruled by the ethics of the military code. They lived by the rule book.'

With the war over, there was more contact between the camp and the outside world. Prisoners volunteered

174

to work on local farms to get outside the hated barbed wire, and there was the strange sight of generals delivering milk in Bridgend. Occasionally they encountered some hostility when they were put to work with British ex-servicemen, newly returned to civilian life, and the mutual antipathy showed itself in small but irritating ways. There was the day that a former U-boat commander tossed stooks of corn at his workmate just a little too hard for comfort, so that the ex-Tommy catching them lost his temper and the two men nearly came to blows. They were separated by one of the senior German officers, who were quick to stamp on any trouble, knowing it could be the end of outside working parties. On the whole, however, there was little trouble. The local farmers were glad to have the help of the Germans, who worked industriously and were often from farming backgrounds themselves. 'One thing that was typical of them stands out in my mind,' said Mrs Mary Board, of Tyla Farm, Merthyr Mawr. 'They were sawing wood one day with a cross-cut saw, one man at each end, and they worked out the number of strokes they needed when the saw was sharp and the number when it was blunt. They were very thorough.' Their old-world courtesy impressed her, too. 'Whenever I came back from town with some shopping they ran to help me – they wouldn't let me carry anything. And General Dittmar would always click his heels at me when we met.'

It was a Merthyr Mawr farmer, Jack Fowler, who invited four German officers to Christmas dinner. 'They arrived in full dress uniform, with their medals. It was a sight to see.' A few days later they sent Mrs Fowler a little jewel box made by a fellow-prisoner: 'a small and modest souvenir with our best thanks for your kindness and all the troubles you took about us,' said the accompanying letter. This particular manifestation of the Christmas spirit by the Fowlers, however, did not meet with the full approval of the local community. 'Some people didn't like it at all,' said Jack.

Many of the Germans attended Nolton Church, and just before they were repatriated Rundstedt presented the rector with a crucifix and a carving of the head of Christ. Rundstedt, in fact, is remembered affectionately by local people as well as by former prisoners. 'He was a real gent,' said Elwyn Davies, who was the official photographer at the camp. 'If you met him three times a day, he always insisted on shaking hands.' Others remember the German brass hats picking dandelions in the country lanes to make dandelion tea, a gentle pastime contrasting strangely with the iron-and-blood philosophy of their military life.

There were artistic prisoners who painted beautiful country scenes on the walls of their huts, but some of their compatriots had more practical hobbies. They carved toys out of wood, and found a market for them in the surrounding village. Ken Jenkins, who was an apprentice bricklayer at the time, was one of the civilians who went into the camp on contract work, and he soon realised that he could do himself a bit of good and make the local kids happy by acting as a go-between. 'Toys were very short then and there was a big demand for the ones the Germans turned out because, let's face it, they were beautifully made. All the people in the village ordered them. I was giving the Germans twenty cigarettes for them and selling them for the price of sixty.' Some of the guards got in on the act too, Fred Allsop for one. 'We gave them Park Drives or Woodbines for the toys at first, but they got wise to that,' he said. 'They insisted on big cigarettes, not small ones.'

All this, of course, was strictly on the Q.T., because any kind of barter with the prisoners of war was strictly forbidden. The farmers weren't allowed to pay them for their services, but they showed their appreciation by plying them with cigarettes and giving them food to supplement their rations. The higher-ranking officers were regarded as social acquisitions by people who saw themselves as leaders of local society, and some were allowed out to accept invitations to tea.

The business of repatriation was slow – painfully slow for the prisoners. It was the summer of 1948, when Lindwall and Miller were pounding the cricket pitches of England and Bradman was making his final Test appearance, before Island Farm ceased to be a prisoner-of-war camp. As the train stood at Bridgend station waiting to take the last men away, the stationmaster made a friendly speech over the loudspeaker wishing them bon voyage. 'Everybody cheered,' said a man who remembers it, 'as if they were holidaymakers.'

The last man to quit the camp was a German NCO

who married a Welsh girl and now lives happily in the Vale of Glamorgan and counts himself as British as the next man. 'I remember walking out and looking over my shoulder just in case someone was calling me back. It was marvellous. To be free. It was like being reborn. If you have never had a taste of captivity you wouldn't know. When you're a prisoner you don't have a name. You're a number. It does something to you. You become soulless. You like to feel you are a somebody, yet everyone tells you you're a nobody. Believe me, after so many years you begin to think you are a nobody . . . Yes, when they let me out at last I ran across the road. Just to be out of sight of the camp.'

POSTSCRIPT

And that should have been that. But Island Farm prison camp refused to die. The actions of a single night in 1945 served to give it a strange permanence, long after its ugly concrete slabs had ceased to perform any useful purpose. It was as if that break for freedom, however brief the liberty of its perpetrators, had somehow endowed the site with a significance which those responsible for its future found puzzling and frustrating. Incredibly, nearly fifty years passed before all but one of the huts were swept away. And even then the question remained: have we done the right thing?

After the departure of the last high-ranking German officers in June 1948, the 26-acre site slumped into limbo. It was expected to become farmland again, but fate decreed otherwise. It became a place for walking the dog and exploring the slowly-disintegrating huts, some of which held artistic treasures. When I first visited Island Farm for a series of newspaper articles in 1970, I was amazed by the beauty and intricacy of the wall paintings left behind by the prisoners. They depicted not only shapely Teutonic ladies but natural beauty of other kinds – landscapes and seascapes, flowers and birds – as well as scenes of urban life. These murals were flaking away, amid the damp and squalor of the long-abandoned huts. It seemed to me a wicked waste not only of artistic endeavour but of historically important items. I wrote to the Imperial War

Museum suggesting that they take an active interest in their preservation, but received a dusty answer. There were plenty such artefacts around, I was told. My view was that if these had been the work of French prisoners in the Napoleonic Wars, a very different view would be taken. Fortunately, the former Mid Glamorgan County Council, who by the early 1990s were the owners of the site, proved to be greater visionaries than the Imperial War Museum. They enlisted the services of the Eighth Wall Art Conservation Society (EWACS), a voluntary group of enthusiasts whose name derives from their interest in the history and artefacts of the United States Eighth Army Air Force. As Neil Sumner, then conservation architect with Mid Glamorgan County Council, notes in his comprehensive and thought-provoking dissertation *Island Farm Prisoner of War Camp, Bridgend: A Conservation Dilemma,* written in 1995: 'Much of their previous work had concerned the removal and conservation of paintings made by American air force men at bases in East Anglia, but they took on the task of assisting the conservation of German artworks with relish. Over several weekends in October 1992 and April 1994, they removed a total of 28 paintings and texts, 26 of which were Germanic in origin.' (The other two might have been the work of American troops billeted in the huts before they housed POWs.) Considering that they had been in dilapidated huts exposed to all weathers for nearly half a century, the rescued paintings were in remarkably good condition. This was due to lucky chance: the whitewashing of many walls, either in 1945 or shortly after the camp's closure. 'This served to protect the fragile pictures beneath from attack by weather and vandals,' Mr Sumner explains. Unhappily, some pictures he had thought worth conserving when he first saw them in 1991 had to be abandoned to the contractor hired to demolish the huts three years later. The preserved paintings are now safely stored away, awaiting a decision on what is to happen to the only remaining evidence that a POW Camp once stood here: Hut 9, where the escape tunnel began.

The demolition of all but the escape hut in the spring of 1994 was the culmination of a long series of proposals and counter-proposals. Conflicting ideas were argued with great passion. There was the 'back to nature' school which favoured the destruction of all the huts to return the site to a state of pastoral quietude: a case strengthened by its proximity to the thatched-cottage serenity of Merthyr Mawr village and the sand dunes beyond. Their ideas were countered by those who saw the continued existence of the huts, however slummy, as offering a gilded opportunity for creating something of permanent value at Island Farm: a tourist and educational attraction centred on the drama of the escape. And then there were the arguments of the 'practical' people in public life who were impatient of the past and looked to what they saw as the future: the creation of a 'science park' for high technology and manufacture which would help to stimulate economic growth in one of Britain's most depressed regions.

According to their reckoning, the former POW camp should make up nearly one-third of the 84 acres needed for their pet project. Many local people were unimpressed: when consulted on the draft plan, the community council wryly observed that 'residents would far prefer the hidden prisoner-of-war camp to a developed industrial area.'

What complicated the issue was the fact that in March 1990, just before a public inquiry into the future of the site, Hut 9 had become a Grade 2 listed building on the grounds that it was of historical importance. This decision by the Secretary of State for Wales followed representations to Cadw, the body responsible for safeguarding Welsh 'heritage' sites, by sympathetic staff in the planning departments of local authorities involved in the web of decision-making around Island Farm. Their view was not shared by everyone, as there were those who agreed with the local councillor who held that the camp 'should have been bulldozed on VE Day.' Even those intrigued by the camp's history often needed convincing that a derelict concrete hut should share official listing with churches, houses and other buildings of architectural merit. Aesthetic considerations, however, played no part whatever in the decision: Hut 9's association with the escape was the sole criterion. The tunnel through which the men crawled to freedom, however, was afforded no official protection, which some thought inconsistent. 'I thought it preposterous,' Neil Sumner writes, 'that the very element which qualified a building to be listed should itself be denied statutory protection. I argued that as a man-made structure it was no different in essence from, say, an Iron Age earthwork, and suggested that consideration could have been given to designating the escape tunnel a scheduled monument. I was informed that scheduling had been considered, but at the time it did not meet the "national importance" criterion.'

All through the 1990s and into the first decade of the 21st century, arguments continued to swirl over what should be done about the slowly decaying remnants of the old POW camp. The case for turning Island Farm into a tourist or educational attraction was argued strongly, the best option appearing to be the preservation of Hut 9 and some of the huts near it. An example of what could be done existed in North Yorkshire, where Eden Camp visitor attraction portrayed the ordinary experience of civilians and service men and women as well as prisoners in World War Two. But in Bridgend, the waters were muddied by conflicting interests, indifference and downright opposition. 'Anyone who wants to go and see a place where people were incarcerated is quite frankly sick,' one councillor declared, while another feared it would become 'a place of pilgrimage for neo-Nazis.' The destruction of every building save Hut 9, a body blow for all but the most modest tourism initiatives, went ahead without a murmur from Cadw or the National Assembly's historic buildings agency. Cadw did, however, make a financial contribution to repairs to Hut 9, the work including the installation of replica steel windows throughout the hut by Bridgend County Borough Council in 1997. As nature reclaimed the camp site, the hut was sealed off behind a high fence but sporadic acts of vandalism occurred. In 2003, planning permission was granted for the Island Farm site to become part of a 'development' taking in new businesses – an extension of the science park – new houses, an hotel and a rugby academy aimed at 'establishing Wales once again as one of the world's leading rugby nations.' Patrons of the hotel would have a fine view of Hut 9, for which a meaningful future had still to be devised.

Over the years, I have been back to Island Farm many times to be interviewed about the escape by journalists and broadcasters. One such occasion was in the summer of 2001, when author Byron Rogers decided to see the place for himself. In a four-page spread in *Saga* magazine headlined *The Great Escape . . . in Wales*, he calls it 'the most forgotten story of the Second World War.'

'It is now 56 years later,' he writes, 'and I have travelled 180 miles to see what remains of the old camp at Island Farm at the side of the A48 on the Porthcawl road, just before the turn to Merthyr Mawr. Now owned by Bridgend County Borough Council, this consists of undergrowth into which, at one point, mysterious stone steps disappear, as though leading to some lost temple. The council has put up a large hopeful sign – "To let, Modern Business Space." With this in mind it has razed the old prison huts, with a single exception, the one from which the tunnel started. I have heard strange stories about this hut.

'That the tunnel is still there . . . That the entrance to it in the hut survives, under some wall-paintings of half-naked women put up to distract the guards. That its exit is where it always was, hidden by undergrowth in a nearby field. Even more bizarre, the excavated earth is still in the hut. *Everything, with the exception of the guards and the escapees, is still there.* You just imagine what a tourist trap anyone with half a brain could make of this frozen moment beside an arterial road . . .

'And it is just as Herbert Williams told me it would be, the fading pictures on the walls, the great mound of earth from the tunnel still in the shower room. Long passageways, rooms on either side. Dust and damp. Nothing has changed . . . This is an amazing place.'

Amazing indeed. But at the time of writing this Postcript, it looked as if a glorious opportunity had been missed to create something of exceptional value here. Certainly not a celebration of incarceration; still less a monument to Nazism; but a resource that would reflect the experiences of prisoners of war the world over, and the physical and mental privations that war continues to inflict on humanity.

Herbert Williams,
April 2004

Also by Herbert Williams

Poetry

Too Wet for the Devil
The Dinosaurs
A Lethal Kind of Love
The Trophy
Ghost Country
Looking Through Time

Novels

A Severe Case of Dandruff
The Woman in Back Row
Punters

Short Stories

The Stars In Their Courses
Stories of King Arthur (for children)

Biography

Davies the Ocean: Railway King and Coal Tycoon
John Cowper Powys

Other Non-Fiction

Stage Coaches in Wales
Railways in Wales
Battles in Wales
Voices of Wales
The Pembrokeshire Coast National Park

Gomer and the Second World War

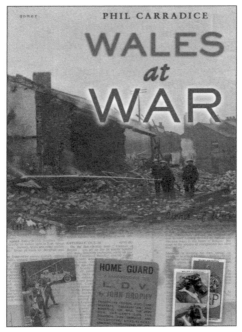

This book tells the stories of those men and women who never appear in the history textbooks. *Wales at War* gives voice to ordinary Welsh people who lived through the Second World War, and who have quite extraordinary stories to relate.

Factory workers, Land Army girls, air-raid wardens, evacuees, firemen, prisoners of war, conscientious objectors, servicemen: all of these people have memories of particular intensity. Their readiness to share their experiences with author Phil Carradice has led to a book that is rich in detail and absolutely authentic in the attitudes and emotions it contains.

ISBN 1 84323 321 5   £9.99

Gomer and the Second World War

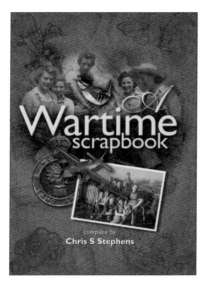

'Being a war baby was just hard luck' – or was it? Children growing up in wartime were certainly kept busy. They could be building a shelter, Digging for Victory in an allotment, taking a day off school for potato-picking, even befriending an evacuee. They had tasks to do - because many fathers were away at war and mothers working in weapons factories or perhaps driving lorries.

A Wartime Scrapbook will give children of the twenty-first century a vivid picture of the Second World War. It is a book for whole families to explore together, especially if grandparents or elderly relatives have memories of their own to share.

Chris Stephens, author of the popular anthologies *A Christmas Box* and *A Seaside Treat*, once again brings social history to life for readers of all ages.

Softback ISBN 1 84323 285 5   £5.99
Hardback ISBN 1 84323 390 8   £8.99